CRIPPLE CREEK
Then and Now
By
ROBERT L. BROWN

WESTERN HISTORY DEPARTMENT, DENVER PUBLIC LIBRARY.

ALTHOUGH THE PHANTOM CANYON tracks were abandoned in 1912, the Florence and Cripple Creek continued operating between Cripple Creek and Victor until 1917.

CRIPPLE CREEK
Then and Now
By
ROBERT L. BROWN

CRIPPLE CREEK
Then and Now
By
ROBERT L. BROWN

250 Broadway • Denver, Colorado 80203

Published by Sundance Publications, Limited
Denver, Colorado 80203

Graphical Presentation and Printing by —
Sundance Publications, Limited, Denver, Colorado

Typesetting by —
LaserWriting, Inc., Denver, Colorado

Copyright © 1991 by Sundance Publications, Limited,
Denver, Colorado 80203. Printed in U.S.A.
All rights reserved. This book, or parts thereof,
may not be reproduced in any form without
written permission of the publisher.

ISBN – 0-913582-52-2

First Printing — May 1991

FRONT COVER; FROM THE COLLECTION OF EVELYN AND ROBERT L. BROWN

IN THIS SCENE we are looking east along Bennett Avenue in Cripple Creek. Note that the Midland Terminal Depot had not appeared as yet at the end of the street. The Palace Hotel, where Sam Strong was killed, shows on the left, in the middle distance. Note also the 25 c. and the 50 c. rates at the Mount Pisgah House, at the extreme right.

THIS COLOR PICTURE looks east on Bennett Avenue. Although the Mount Pisgah House and the Palace are gone, the Midland Terminal Depot shows at the end of the street. The Midland Terminal Depot now houses the District Museum. FROM THE COLLECTION OF EVELYN AND ROBERT L. BROWN

ROBERT L. BROWN

FOR MANY YEARS, Robert L. Brown has been gathering detailed information and material for his books about the American West — including countless color transparencies. His efforts in this respect have taken him to literally hundreds of ghost towns and historic sites throughout the West.

Mr. Brown's teaching experience includes the University of Denver, the Denver Public Schools and the University of Colorado. His teaching areas are Western History and the History of Colorado.

He has written seven books to date, including "SALOONS OF THE AMERICAN WEST" and "AN EMPIRE OF SILVER." Three are concerned with ghost towns and are titled "Jeep Trails to Colorado Ghost Towns," "Ghost Towns of the Colorado Rockies," and "Colorado Ghost Towns, Past and Present." "Holy Cross, the Mountain and the City" and "An Empire of Silver" are regional histories. "Uphill Both Ways" concerns Colorado's hiking trails and was published in 1976.

Mr. Brown holds memberships in the Colorado Authors League, Western Writers of America, and he served as Sheriff of the Denver Posse of the Westerners in 1969. In spare moments, he records talking books for the Colorado State Library for the Blind. Both Robert L. Brown and his wife, Evelyn, are active members of the Colorado Mountain Club.

FROM THE COLLECTION OF EVELYN AND ROBERT L. BROWN

IN COLORADO SPRINGS, Pikes Peak Avenue runs directly east and west, providing and unobstructed view of the famous mountain. In the middle distance, the large structure is the original Antlers Hotel.

DEDICATION

For Diana and Marshall, our daughter and son, that they too may enjoy what man and nature have wrought in Colorado's Pikes Peak Region.

ACKNOWLEDGEMENTS

IN PREPARING ANY BOOK the writer incurs many debts. First of all, special gratitude is due my wife and best friend for more than four decades, Evelyn McCall Brown. She was my companion on all of our treks to the Cripple Creek country, assisting in the research and with pictures. For the tenth time Freda and Francis B. Rizzari have proofread a completed manuscript for me. Someone told me some years ago that a successful proofreader need to know more about the subject than the author. The Rizzaris fit that description, and I thank them for their competence and for many suggestions.

Unless indicated otherwise, the majority of the photographs have come from our personal collection. The Rizzaris supplied many others. The late Fred and Jo Mazzulla made dozens of prints available before their collection was sold. The Western History Department of the Denver Public Library, where the majority of my research was done, supplied a number of other pictures. Mrs. Eleanor Gehres and her able staff were of great assistance. The library at the Colorado Heritage Center assisted with other inquiries and pictures. Nancy and Edwin Bathke of Manitou Springs hiked the original Ute Trail with us on two occasions and supplied a couple of rare photographs as well.

My long-time good friend, Jack L. Morison, was my companion on my first exposure to Cripple Creek, many years ago. We approached the district through a snowstorm, and it was just a great day. The parents and grandparents of another good friend, Donald J. Moser, owned and operated a market and a theater in Cripple Creek. Don has been most generous about sharing the memories of his family with me.

In common with others who have researched the Cripple Creek saga, the most perplexing problem has been that people who knew Cripple Creek in its latter days do not agree about what happened, where and sometimes even to whom. For many years, a Cripple Creek Pioneers group met annually in Denver's Washington Park. "Outsiders" were discouraged. My sources report that much time was spent disagreeing with each other over historical details. Whenever possible, several sources that agree have been utilized in an effort to be as accurate as possible. All "stories" have been identified as such.

Even the gold-production statistics vary widely from one source to another. The fact that Cripple Creek's story extends well into the present century is possibly the source of the problem. We are even now too close to it for an objective view. Time may afford us a better perspective.

For those persons who may wish to pursue the Cripple Creek narrative further, in my opinion, the finest single-volume work on this subject is Marshall Sprague's monumental ***Money Mountain***, listed in the accompanying bibliography. I regard it as the definitive source and refer to it constantly.

For pinpointing specific locations I recommend the U.S. Geological Survey quadrangle map of 1906, reprinted in 1925. Ask for the Colorado, (Teller County) Cripple Creek Quadrangle. The 1951 Cripple Creek North and South Quadrangles are larger, and they are also very good.

To all of the foregoing persons, sources and institutions, my heartfelt thanks.

R.L.B.

INTRODUCTION

COLORADO'S CRIPPLE CREEK Mining District was an incredible place, by nearly any standard that can be applied. First of all, it occurred within the six-square-mile crater of an extinct volcano, which probably had an unsymmetrical conal shape. It was located just beyond the west shoulder of America's best-known mountain, 14,110 foot high Pikes Peak. Prior to the 1890's, most of the respected mining theories held that precious metals such as gold or silver do not occur in lava complexes. But this one was different! Pikes Peak's south slope occupied the ground floor of the extinct volcano, and somewhere deep down in the Earth's core, the erupting cauldron had apparently gathered great quantities of molten gold into its stew. A series of eruptions carried the gold-impregnated lava materials to the surface, leaving them exposed as tellurides of lava. As a consequence, many previously authoritative textbooks needed to be revised.

Because of its peculiar geological structure, the Pikes Peak Region was considered to be worthless for mining prospects. It flourished as a hay ranch for a time and as a timberline cow pasture, where a handful of ranches survived. Due to its location in a recessed bowl, which afforded protection from icy winter winds, the cold months were usually fairly mild.

When gold was found in California during 1849, one of the better routes to the Pacific Coast followed the well-established Northern Branch of the Santa Fe Trail up the Arkansas River to a point about five miles west of Bent's Fort. There, the migrants turned toward the northwest, following alongside the eastern foothills of the Front Range of the Rockies, past Pikes Peak. Continuing northward, the trail intersected the California and Oregon trails, in what is now Wyoming. Lots of those who located no gold in California, trickled homeward by reversing the same route. Only an optimistic few among them considered trying their luck around Pikes Peak.

Then, in 1859, the drama was replayed, when a modest quantity of gold was found about ten miles south of the confluence of Cherry Creek and the South Platte River, within contemporary Denver. Those men and women who sought precious metals in the West were nearly always from somewhere else. Colorado Territory, in its beginning, was not old enough to have produced native sons or daughters. The Indians and those who lived in a handful of Spanish-Mexican settlements in the lower San Luis Valley were exceptions. Most of the Anglo-Americans who migrated to the West were from small towns or farms, and they brought hometown habits and customs with them.

Although there were other ways to reach the goldfields of western Kansas, now part of Colorado, once again, would-be prospectors ascended the Arkansas River path and turned toward the northwest, beyond the now crumbling remains of Bent's Fort. By this time, the cutoff had acquired a title, the Old Cherokee Trail, named for the Cherokee people from Georgia and Oklahoma, who had used this path 10 years earlier as a shortcut between the Santa Fe and Oregon-California trails. Since few other landmarks were known at that time, and because the route passed by the mountain, the entire 1859 gold excitement came to be known as the Pikes Peak Gold Rush.

There are records of prospectors who sought gold around Fountain Creek and of others who ascended Ute Pass looking for the yellow metal while on their way to South Park. Curiously, in 1859, they largely ignored the region which would become know as Cripple Creek.

For the next several years, it was gold in the Rockies that induced large numbers of Eastern victims of the Panic of 1857 (an economic depression) to move west. Currently, at this point in time, many of the so-called authorities felt that the best gold deposits in western Kansas had been tapped and depleted.

Then, in the 1870's, the pendulum swung to silver. A series of rich strikes were made around Aspen, Leadville, in the San Juan Mountains, and finally, at Creede.

Meanwhile, the ill-starred Mount Pisgah Hoax of 1884 resulted in a brief flurry of excitement over an alleged gold discovery in the neighborhood of Cripple Creek. Since the Mount Pisgah affair was only a "salted" claim, contrived solely to line the pockets of a few con men, the hoax served only to disparage the future reputation of the region among mining men.

But all of this changed in 1891. There really was gold at Pikes Peak! Before it was finished, Cripple Creek had become the second-greatest gold-producing region of the world. It was out-produced only by the great Witwatersrand fields of the Transvaal in South Africa. However, for any of the years it was going, Cripple Creek outstripped the Witwatersrand, but the the Transvaal location continued to produce for a greater number of years, leaving Cripple Creek in second place in terms of total production.

By 1899, Cripple Creek's gold output amounted to one-fourth of all the gold produced in the United States and two-thirds of all that was mined in Colorado. As noted in the acknowledgements, accurate figures are difficult to find with reference to Cripple Creek's total gold production. Usually reliable sources vary widely. A conservative, safe ball-park figure would be something in excess of $250 million. This figure, it should be remembered, is for gold that was priced at only $20 an ounce, whereas today's going rate is over $300 per ounce. Silver and copper recovery would expand this production figure, as would amounts from high-grading, which was never reported. To put it into perspective, gold from Cripple Creek alone exceeded by at least 50 percent the total for gold recovered in all of California's Mother Lode Country.

CRIPPLE CREEK MUSEUM COLLECTION

TABLE OF CONTENTS

Chapter		Page
1.	Cripple Creek's Geography	11
2.	Zebulon Pike and His Peak	15
3.	Before the Gold	23
4.	The Mount Pisgah Hoax	27
5.	Bob Womack and the El Paso Lode	29
6.	Hayden Placer, Fremont and Cripple Creek	33
7.	Winfield Scott Stratton	39
8.	Life Among the Miners	45
9.	The Iron Horse Comes to Cripple Creek	57
10.	The Midland Terminal Arrives	71
11.	Cripple Creek's Short Line	75
12.	The Fires	83
13.	Labor Wars at the Turn of the Century	93
14.	Cripple Creek Personalities	101
15.	Cripple Creek's Satellites	107
16.	Victor and its Neighbors	121
17.	The Bowl of Gold in the 20th Century	126

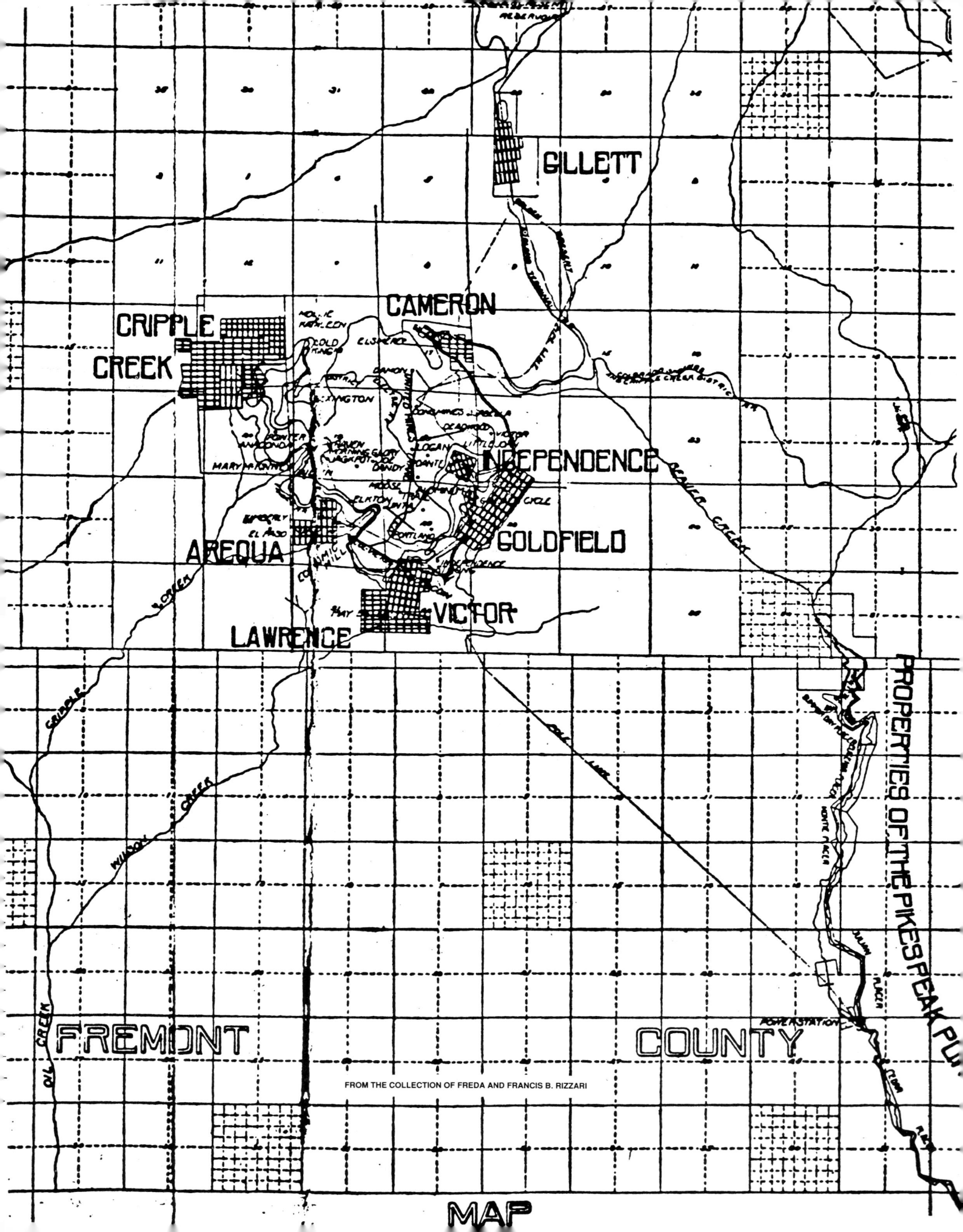

Cripple Creek's Geography

IN THE BEGINNING, the land that is now Colorado, was a vast nearly level plain, which supported lush tropical plants in a moist rain forest climate. At that time, it was home to several species of reptile life, the dinosaurs whose skeletal remains are still found. More than 300 million years ago, a vast shallow salty arm of the Pacific Ocean moved inland and covered much of the Great Plains, eastward into contemporary Kansas. Even today, salt-water sea shells can be seen in Glenwood Canyon, among other places. Salt deposits of the inland sea still exist, near the town of Morrison and in South Park.

Our first mountain range was pushed up from the earth's crust by volcanic pressure. Initially, the range was higher than our present mountains until it was gradually worn down by centuries of glacial action, as well as by wind and water erosion. Our current Rocky Mountains appeared about 25 million years ago and appear to be still growing, but only very slowly.

The year 1874 brought the prestigious Hayden Survey to Colorado Territory. Its purpose was to examine and measure this segment of the Rocky Mountain chain, especially the higher peaks. Among the scientific personnel who accompanied Hayden were several geologists. After exploring the Cripple Creek basin, they described it as "...a volcanic region containing a dirty gray rock called trachorheite, probably sylvanite."

During the Tertiary period, some 10 to 55 million years ago, a series of powerful explosions occurred. This resulted in a shattering of the Earth's granite crust, a material that is common to Colorado's Rockies. These volcanic activities began an inevitable pushing up of the Earth's crust. The late Professor Henry Lamb of Colorado College (in Colorado Springs) identified Pikes Peak as one of the centers of volcanic disturbance. "When the eruption occurred," he wrote, "boiling hot water from deep in the Earth percolated to the surface, carrying gold tellurides in a salt solution mixed with quartz and lava. As the substance was disbursed, molten gold was caught in the cracks."

There was not just a single explosion, but a whole series of massive eruptions that built up a cone. Then came lesser explosions, creating a network of channels, which carried the gold-bearing masses to the surface. Gradually, a broad crater-like basin took shape, a caldera, formed either by the explosion or by the collapse of the cone. Estimates suggest that the main crater was at least 5,000 feet deep. Minor craters occurred at nearby Globe Hill and on Beacon Hill, among other locations.

One side effect of Cripple Creek's story is the often-heard suggestion that Pikes Peak was originally much higher than its current 14,110 feet. When the volcano erupted, Pikes Peak lost several hundred feet in the process. Since no human beings were here to gauge the event, who can say what really happened?

As the volcanic activity subsided, the Cripple Creek cone was filled up with materials from deep within the earth. This latter process continued over a period of several millennia. As minor eruptions continued, silver, copper and more gold were deposited in the form of tellurides within the narrow fissures, where gradual cooling took place. Most of the veins were thin, and only a few were broad.

The gold was in the form of sylvanite and calaverite. Sylvanite was first found in Transylvania (in eastern Europe), and it is described as being gray or silvery telluride of gold, mixed with silver. Calaverite is a native American telluride of gold, containing some silver. It was named for Calaveras County, California, where it was initially discovered and identified.

Many centuries later, when the source of Cripple Creek's gold had been determined and understood, the whole mining district acquired the nickname of "The Bowl of Gold." Because of its peculiar geological structure, the name has persisted to this day.

WILLIAM H. JACKSON PHOTO – COLLECTION OF RICHARD RONZIO

THE INCOMPARABLE William Henry Jackson, the American West's finest photographer, exposed this fine glass-plate negative during one of his many Colorado tours. The subject shows Pikes Peak, with the Garden of the Gods in the foreground. The rock formation called the "Kissing Camels" appears at the upper right in this historic view.

FROM THE COLLECTION OF EVELYN AND ROBERT L. BROWN

FROM THE 14,110-FOOT-HIGH SUMMIT of Pikes Peak, this is the view which inspired Katharine Lee Bates to compose the libretto of America the Beautiful. Just the edge of Cripple Creek is visible in the middle distance, while Mount Pisgah shows at the extreme right.

COLLECTION OF FRED AND JO MAZZULLA

SINCE PHOTOGRAPHS were unknown in his lifetime, we have only the work of contemporary artists to portray the likeness of Lieutenant Zebulon Montgomery Pike. This drawing is the most widely credited likeness of the U.S. Army explorer.

Zebulon Pike and His Grand Peak

RIPPLE CREEK'S location is below the west side of the peak that has been described as America's Most Famous Mountain. It drew both its name and fame from Colorado's first official explorer, Lieutenant Zebulon Montgomery Pike, a career soldier and West Point graduate. The military tradition was strong in the family. Pike's father had risen to the rank of general.

In 1806, Lieutenant Pike was named to lead an expedition to check out some of that portion of the Louisiana Purchase that had not been covered by explorers Lewis and Clark. During earlier years, both Spain and France had claimed the area, but neither power did anything with it.

General James Wilkinson, one of the ranking scoundrels of American history, was Pike's immediate superior, and he was the person responsible for choosing the young lieutenant as the party's leader. President Thomas Jefferson's knowledge of the expedition was only casual. Wilkinson was the other half of the odious Burr-Wilkinson scheme, which would have stolen a substantial tract of land in the American Southwest in order to start their own country. Probably because of "guilt by association," later historians were troubled by the notion that Pike could have been a part of the conspiracy. Subsequent research has completely exonerated the young officer. Lieutenant Pike was clean!

Pike's orders were to ascend the Arkansas River to its source, presumably in the so-called "Mexican Mountains," today's Rockies. At that point, the party was to proceed south along the Continental Divide to the source of the Red River, which was to be followed back to civilization.

Since the Red River does not originate in the Rockies, the plan was not possible. Nevertheless, Pike and his men started out from Fort Belle Fontaine, above St. Louis, ascending the Missouri River before crossing overland to the Arkansas. Pike and his party of 22 men entered what is now eastern Colorado at 2:00 p.m. on November 15, 1806.

Pike first observed a great snowy mountain mass from a high point of land near La Junta, or possibly further upstream. His journals record that he mistook the peak for a small blue cloud on the horizon. However, the "blue cloud" was still there the following day, and the next. With eyes trained for the lower Alleghenies, Pike possibly became the first victim of a common Colorado illusion. He wrote in his journal that "Grand Peak [as Pike had chosen to call it] might be as much as fifteen miles away." Their actual distance was in excess of 100 miles at that time. Pike also recorded in his journal that the mountain's altitude was 18,581 feet, an error that he never corrected.

Soon, the men were using the peak as a landmark, heading generally northwest toward it. November found the explorers close to the present sites of either Cañon City or Pueblo. Authorities differ on the location, but agree that the men made camp and remained there for two weeks. Still deceived by distances, Pike and three men left the camp on November 24 "...to take the afternoon off for a climb of Grand Peak." Typically, the military had outfitted the late-autumn expedition with summer-weight clothing. Pike and his men suffered from bitter cold during their attempted climb.

Their route followed present Colorado Highway 15 north from a point close to today's city of Florence to just south of Colorado Springs, where they began climbing. Soon, it began to snow, and they spent an uncomfortable night in a cave. It was Thanksgiving, but they felt there was little to be thankful for. Finally, they "cliffed out" on either Cheyenne Mountain or, more probably, on nearby Miller Mountain. Again, sources differ. Because Pike still held to his 18,581-foot altitude estimate, he wrote in his journal that "...probably no man would ever climb to its summit." That afternoon hike had now stretched into six days. Historian Marshall Sprague noted that this side expedition made Pike forever famous as the first American who never climbed Pikes Peak.

From their camp, the party ascended Currant Creek to South Park, where they spent the first Christmas ever celebrated by Americans in Colorado. The site of their holiday observance is near present-day Salida. They crossed Trout Creek Pass to the Arkansas Valley, follow-

WESTERN HISTORY DEPARTMENT – DENVER PUBLIC LIBRARY

THIS EARLY VIEW shows the depot and ticket office at the end of Ruxton Avenue in Manitou Springs. This is the starting point for passengers riding the Manitou & Pikes Peak Railway, the famous cog-wheel line that ascends Pikes Peak.

THIS COLOR PICTURE shows how little things have changed since the earlier view was taken. The Manitou & Pikes Peak building still retains its original charm. Thousands of tourists ride the little red trains of this unusual railroad.

FROM THE COLLECTION OF EVELYN AND ROBERT L. BROWN

WESTERN HISTORY DEPARTMENT – DENVER PUBLIC LIBRARY

FROM THE LITTLE DEPOT in Manitou Springs, this view looks up along the stone wall and the rack-and-pinion tracks at the beginning of the renowned Manitou & Pikes Peak Railway.

THIS COLOR VIEW portrays the identical masonry wall and tracks from the Manitou & Pikes Peak Railway depot in Manitou Springs. This historic terminal is near the upper end of Ruxton Avenue.

FROM THE COLLECTION OF EVELYN AND ROBERT L. BROWN

FROM THE COLLECTION OF EVELYN AND ROBERT L. BROWN

IN THIS PICTURE we see the village of Manitou Springs as it appeared during the days of the Cripple Creek gold excitement.

MANITOU SPRINGS, was widely known for its many soda springs, which were popular with health-seekers. Several are still active. The Cliff House was just one of the numerous hostelries that catered to those who came to "take the waters," as it was called then, or to ride the "Cog Wheel Route" up Pikes Peak.

FROM THE COLLECTION OF EVELYN AND ROBERT L. BROWN

CLIFF HOUSE AND MANITOU SODA SPRINGS

FROM THE COLLECTION OF EVELYN AND ROBERT L. BROWN

THIS WAS THE FIRST TRAIN to reach the summit of Pikes Peak. The angle of the locomotive corresponds to the angle of most of the railroad grade, thus assuring that the water in the boiler will remain level. The observation cars were pushed upgrade by the locomotives.

ing the river deep into the gorge. Pike's party emerged about where the Royal Gorge cable car operates today, before returning to their base camp, near present-day Cañon City. Turning to the southwest, they probably crossed Mosca Pass to the broad San Luis Valley. There, they erected a log fortification. Here, Pike apparently mistook the Conejos River for the elusive Red River, wandered into Spanish territory and was arrested by Spaniards. The Spanish troopers took the best horses and gave Pike's men the poorer ones. They also kept Pike's notes, except for those he was able to hide inside a rifle barrel. New Spain's officials were unable to decide if Pike was a spy or not, and the party was released to return home the next spring.

By 1812, the United States was involved in its second war with Great Britain. Pike was a lieutenant no longer, having been field-commissioned as a brigadier general. In the charge on York, he and most of those under his command were killed. Pike was only 34 years of age at the time of his death. Unfortunately, he did not live to hear his mountain called Pikes Peak. The name gained favor with later map makers, who renamed Grand Peak in honor of the late Zebulon M. Pike.

Because of the economics of the War of 1812, there was a slight dip in America's financial status, a mild depression. Under such circumstances, items such as exploration, especially military expeditions, became a low priority. No official explorers entered the West again until 1820, when Major Stephen H. Long was sent out to complete the work that had been interrupted when Pike was taken to the Spanish territorial capital at Santa Fe.

Before embarking on a military career as a cartographer, Stephen Long had been a teacher of mathematics at Dartmouth College. Unlike Pike, his route west followed the Platte River. He mistook the mountain now called Longs Peak for Pikes Peak. Later, he did survey Pikes Peak and the nearby foothills westward toward South Park. Doctor Edwin James, a botanist who accompanied Long, became the first American of record to successfully reach the top of Pikes Peak. However, when he arrived, Edwin James found evidence in a cave that Indians had regarded this as a fine place to snare eagles for the feathers so useful in their ceremonial dances. Unfortunately, there was no way to determine the identity of those native Americans, so Doctor James became the first American of record to reach the summit.

In the intervening years, many traders and trappers sought furs and traded with the Mountain Utes, who had long lived and prospered in this region. In the process, these traders became familiar with the area soon to be known as the Cripple Creek district. Curiously, traders and trappers had almost no interest in precious metals. As a prisoner in Santa Fe, Zebulon Pike had met a trapper named James Purcell, who told of finding gold in South Park. He showed Pike a variety of nuggets he had taken from Tarryall Creek. Then, apparently to show his contempt for anyone who was not a trapper, Purcell threw the samples away. Being illiterate, few trappers left any written records. Fur-company ledgers and the journals of explorers, such as Pike or Long, are among the few available sources.

James Ohio Pattie was in South Park as early as

DELL A. MCCOY PHOTO.

DIESEL ELECTRIC UNITS, purchased from Switzerland, now take sight-seers up to the summit of Pikes Peak.

THIS VIEW OF THE COG RAILWAY, shows people on the rear platform. The view was taken at an altitude of 12,000 feet, as the train assended Pikes Peak thru a snowbank, in early summer.

FROM THE COLLECTION OF EVELYN AND ROBERT L. BROWN

LIBRARY – COLORADO HISTORICAL SOCIETY

IN 1902, THE ST. LOUIS GLOBE DEMOCRAT published this painting of Lieutenant Zebulon Pike and his men viewing the "Great Mountain" from the point where they "cliffed out" and then were forced to turn back.

1827. Upon departing, he moved south, passing close to Cripple Creek as he followed the old original Ute Trail down to the Great Plains. Between 1842 and 1844, John C. Fremont and his party traveled around the base of Pikes Peak, but neither Pattie nor Fremont reported any signs of gold.

In 1893, an exchange teacher of English from Massachusetts, had a room at the Antlers Hotel in Colorado Springs while teaching a class at Colorado College. Her name was Katharine Lee Bates, and she was destined to bring lasting fame to Pikes Peak. On July 22 of 1893, Miss Bates took the well-known trip up from Cascade in a mule-drawn buckboard, or "prairie wagon." Reaching the rocky summit of Pikes Peak was a "must" jaunt for Colorado's visitors at that time. It was a lovely, clear day, and the teacher was greatly impressed by the handsome vistas she observed on all sides. She spent about 30 minutes on the top of the peak.

That evening, while back in her room, she penned the original stanzas for *America the Beautiful,* a lovely song that many Americans today would prefer as the national anthem. Two years later, Katharine Bates re-wrote several of the lines, making them more direct. Samuel A. Ward of New Jersey wrote the familiar music that accompanies the libretto. Katharine Lee Bates undoubtedly looked down into the Cripple Creek basin from the summit, but she had no particular reason to take special notice of it.

However, a scant two years before, in 1891, both the mountain and Cripple Creek had been catapulted into national notoriety by that incredible gold discovery made by an itinerant cattle tender, a cowboy, named Bob Womack.

FROM THE COLLECTION OF EVELYN AND ROBERT L. BROWN

W. E. HOOK OF MANITOU SPRINGS made this remarkably clear picture of the Ute Pass Road to Cripple Creek. In this view, the photographer was looking west from a point at the edge of the popular summer resort of Manitou Springs.

Before the Gold

ESPITE THE EXPLORATIONS of Pike, Long, Fremont, Pattie and others, the Cripple Creek basin remained relatively unknown. At least it was regarded as a region of little interest to the people who had come to the new Colorado Territory. For one thing, the Ute Indians lived in the mountains, and were known to have used Mount Pisgah as a signal mountain. Their artifacts were found there. They were regarded as fierce fighters who guarded their mountain retreats jealously. Physically, the Utes were a small, stocky people, possessed of a somewhat darker skin pigmentation, as compared with those Indians who lived on Colorado's eastern plains.

These slightly different physical characteristics provided adequate reasons for the taller, statuesque Arapaho and Cheyenne Indians to hate the Utes. From infancy, they told their children that the Utes were short, dark-skinned, bow-legged and had disgusting sanitary practices. Furthermore, they spent most of their time running around South Park eating worms, bugs and occasionally each other. No doubt, the Utes related equally ridiculous tale to their offspring concerning the plains people.

At this time, Colorado's high mountain parks (large open valleys) were prime hunting areas, filled with a variety of edible animal life. A huge buffalo herd enjoyed the salt deposits left by the inland sea in South Park. Elk, deer, antelope, bears and other species lived there, too, a situation made to order for the mountain Indian's way of life. Sheer cussedness and perhaps envy motivated the plains Indians to conduct regular forays up through Currant Creek Canyon for hassling the Utes, and to kill buffalo in South Park. For their part, the Utes also had a trail that was useful for forays against the Cheyenne and Arapaho. As one might expect, it was called the Ute Trail.

When the Pikes Peak Gold Rush began in 1859, a small settlement, called El Dorado, was started near the eastern end of the Ute Trail. Soon, the name was changed to Colorado City. As a stimulus to the frantic trade in mining supplies, the business community of Colorado City improved the Ute Trail in 1859 and 1860 for use by prospectors headed for the gold-mining towns in South Park. Some went on from there to Oro City in the upper Arkansas Valley. Augusta Tabor's diary describes how she and her husband, Horace, drove their wagon south from Denver City to Colorado City, then went west over the Ute Trail to Buckskin Joe. Since the trail crossed a range of mountains, people soon began calling it Ute Pass. For the record, the original Ute Pass, now a hiking path, still exists in the next valley south of U.S. Highway 24, today's paved Ute Pass. Although the '59ers bypassed Cripple Creek, for the most part, there were a few exceptions.

Among those who came to the West during the 1859 gold excitement was the family of a widower named Sam Womack. Kentucky had been their home. Sam had two sons, William and Bob. The latter was destined to put what is now Cripple Creek on the map. They arrived in 1861, and proceeded to do some mining in what is now Clear Creek County, west of Denver. By 1867, they had had enough and were ready to move south for a try at cattle ranching. Banker Irving Howbert advised the family to file on some vacant land down on Little Fountain Creek. Sunview Ranch was the name they chose for their new home. There, they raised cattle, while Bob and William learned to ride horses. They stayed until 1871, when their neighboring ranchers, the Weltys, decided that the Colorado City environs were becoming over-populated.

Levi Welty's family had come out from Ohio. Three of their four children were boys. Welty and his brood made their way up Ute Pass into what was then called the West Pikes Peak Country. Levi was impressed with the pretty, steep-walled 9,500-foot-high valley. He envisioned it as a suitable place in which to raise their cattle. They felled trees and erected a log cabin close to the spring, which was the source of the soon-to-be-named Cripple Creek. The name, which has endured, came from a series of misfortunes suffered by animals and people while crossing the stream on algae-coated rocks. There are many versions, some quite humorous, of the accidents that ensued.

FROM THE COLLECTION OF FREDA AND FRANCIS B. RIZZARI

AN UNKNOWN LENSMAN took this very early picture of some of the first residences at Cripple Creek. Notice that some of them are mere tents, while others have canvas roofs.

SHORTLY AFTER his famous discovery of the fabulously-rich El Paso Lode, Bob Womack posed for this photograph in front of his original cabin on the Levi Welty homestead.

LIBRARY – COLORADO HISTORICAL SOCIETY

Following a visit by Bob Womack to the Welty homestead, in company with members of the 1874 Hayden Survey, Bob decided to stay behind and renew his acquaintance with the family. Two years later, the Weltys sold their place to the Womacks for the unlikely sum of $500 and a couple of pigs. Bob filed on an adjacent homestead of his own in Arequa Gulch.

In May of 1878, while tending the family herd, Bob picked up a piece of lightweight material called "float." In Denver it assayed out at $200 to the ton in gold. Bob

COLLECTION OF ED AND NANCY BATHKE
BETWEEN 1896 AND 1920, a lady named Anna Tweed maintained a photographic studio in Colorado Springs. Mrs. Tweed took this remarkable picture showing wagons on the several levels of the "W" on the Pikes Peak wagon road.

was now 30 years old, and was about to embark on a 12-year odyssey to locate the source from which his float rock had broken off. What he needed to find was the gold-laced material that had become embedded in the cracks during that long-ago volcanic eruption. He looked for an outcropping higher up in Poverty Gulch. Centuries of wind and water erosion complicated his quest, as did his continuing-and-distasteful duties tending the family herd. Bob cared little for being a "cattle farmer." Searching for gold was now uppermost in his mind.

Meanwhile, Corella Womack, Bob's stepmother, died in 1879. His father, Sam, quickly lost interest in running cattle at 9,500 feet. Both of the Womack homesteads were sold to a man named Frank Anderson for $5,000. Except for Bob, who chose to remain behind, the rest of the Womack family returned to Kentucky. Frank Anderson formed the Pikes Peak Land & Cattle Company. Later, he sold out to a glove manufacturer, named Philip Ellsworth, for $20,000. Ellsworth, in turn, resold it to the Bennett & Myers Real Estate Company of Denver. During 1885, Bennett & Myers leased the tract to George Carr, a cattleman from Kansas City, for $50 a month. Carr established a "spread" that he called the Broken Box Ranch.

George Carr was a sound businessman who soon had the ranch on a paying basis. Meanwhile, Bob Womack was still living in his cabin in Poverty Gulch. When he asked for a job, Carr hired him, and Bob continued his prosaic search for that elusive gold source. Still, nobody really took Bob seriously. There were two reasons for this: the Mount Pisgah Hoax of 1884 and Bob's long-standing reputation as a many-faceted eccentric.

Early in life, "Cowboy Bob" had acquired a taste for whiskey, and he never handled it very well. Although the family had tried to interest him in the cattle business, Bob enjoyed only the time spent in the saddle, while disdaining other aspects of the work. A clever hiding place was contrived for his liquor supply. It was a hole he had dug above his cabin in Poverty Gulch. While whiskey usually does not set well on the stomach of a rider on a galloping horse, somehow it never affected Bob's horsemanship. While mounted on his horse, Whistler, he gained a reputation as an accomplished master of equine feats, whether intoxicated or otherwise. Once, Bob took the Keeley cure, but it did not last.

When Colorado City's first brothel opened, Womack became so elated that he rode Whistler up the stairs, entered the saloon and demanded that his mount be served a beer. On Saturdays, he usually rode down to Colorado City with the other cowboys for their weekly binge. Children of the town, aware of his reputation, would lie in wait and wager 25 cents with him that he could not shoot out a gaslight from the back of his horse. Bob knew that he could, and he was sometimes arrested and forced to spend a night in the local "slammer," meditating on his costly proficiency.

At other times, Bob won small bets by leaning from the saddle of his galloping horse to pick up a bottle of whiskey with his teeth, within three tries. He usually insisted on drinking the whiskey as a part of the show. Considering the relative hardness of teeth as compared with bottles, this story should probably be discounted.

Bob Womack was a simple, fun-loving soul who rarely thought ahead to the consequences of his actions. There was a gentility in his manner. When arrested for disturbing the peace, or for public drunkenness, he would turn his guileless blue eyes toward the judge, looking as if he were more worried by what his mother would say than by the possible jail sentence he could be facing. And so, Bob's eccentricities did little to improve his social life, or to enhance his reputation as one of the more stable weekend visitors to Colorado City. And then, as if to compound the felony, there came to pass the whole unfortunate business that would be known as the Mount Pisgah Hoax.

FROM THE COLLECTION OF EVELYN AND ROBERT L. BROWN

WILLIAM H. JACKSON, probably the West's finest photographer, exposed this unusually fine view of Cripple Creek in 1900. Mount Pisgah is in the center background.

The Mount Pisgah Hoax

**Y 1884 BUSINESS ACTIVITY** in southern Fremont County had slowed to a trickle. Shopkeeppers were becoming desperate. So, in order to stimulate some trade, a group of Cañon City merchants his upon a devious plan. They hired two slippery operators, named S. J. Bradley and D. G. Miller, to come down from Leadville to salt an 18 foot dry hole with gold-bearing gravel. Bradley and Miller chose the spot on a ranch beside Mount McIntyre, some 13 miles west of Cripple Creek. The Cañon City merchants paid them a paltry $200 for their handiwork. Teller Placer was the name they chose, "honoring" Henry M. Teller, one of Colorado's first pair of United States senators. Although Teller had nothing to do with the plot, people soon began referring to it as the Teller Lode.

Bradley and Miller chose some pretty good stuff, probably from South Park, to dump into that hole. It assayed at $200 to the ton. Down in Cañon City a loquacious promoter, named Captain H. B. Grose, was retained to spread the word by planting stories in Colorado newspapers. But the papers failed to check their facts and got the story all wrong. Almost at once, their headlines screamed about a rich gold find on the east slope of Mount Pisgah, which put the whole thing in the Cripple Creek basin.

Almost alone, Bob Womack saw through the story right away, but nobody would listen because Bob was the town character, an embarrassing local joke some said. Soon, General Palmer's Denver & Rio Grande Railroad had to operate special trains to Cañon City, where eager merchants sold mining supplies and stagecoach tickets to an estimated 50,000 gullible would-be miners, but only a small percentage of the ticket purchasers chose to stay.

Meanwhile, back up at the ranch, now known as "The Mount Pisgah Gold Field", a tent town of "squatters" was growing, complete with saloons, canvas-topped hotels, stores, assay offices, gambling dens, dancehalls and more saloons. Unfortunately, there was no gold beyond that which had been salted in the hole. When it was gone, the perfidy gradually came to light. The only thing that prevented a double hanging was the scarcity of stout trees in this nearly 10,000-foot-high hayfield.

Although the Rio Grande railroad and Cañon City profited, nobody else realized any money from what was quickly labeled "The Mount Pisgah Hoax." Even the name of Mount Pisgah left a bad taste in people's mouths. And when Bob Womack really did find his elusive gold deposit, the news was discounted, due to Womack's reputation as a clown and a drunk. Besides that, the Cripple Creek basin, where "Crazy Bob" made his important find, was just too close to the odious Mount Pisgah.

FROM THE COLLECTION OF FRED AND JO MAZZULLA

DURING THE LATER YEARS of his life, a Cripple Creek photographer took this studio likeness of Robert W. Womack, who made the original gold discovery at Cripple Creek.

Bob Womack and The El Paso Lode

 N OCTOBER 13, 1886, a scant two years after the ill-starred affair at Mount Pisgah, Bob Womack staked-out his first claim, located on the north slope of Poverty Gulch. He called it the Grand View, but he continued hunting for the big one. To support himself and his dreams he still worked cattle for George Carr on the Broken Box Ranch. On those occasions when his charges were quiet, he would take a shovel and pick from his duffel bag to dig prospect holes. Somehow, he never bothered to fill up his excavations again.

George Carr later recalled how he often admonished Bob. "Womack," he would say, "you have to stop digging those holes. Another cow fell in yesterday, broke a leg and had to be destroyed." He usually concluded with a threat of firing Bob unless the digging stopped. But Carr was genuinely fond of his lonely rider. The random excavations continued when Bob thought nobody was watching, and the threatened firing never materialized. From time to time, he returned to the Grand View claim to work around its eastern edge. Meanwhile, on October 20, 1890, he found the outcropping that had eluded him for so long. He named it the El Paso Lode.

Doctor Edward Grannis was a 37 year old tubercular dentist from Ohio who had migrated to Colorado in 1886 to seek the cure. Colorado Springs banker, Irving Howbert, introduced him to Bob Womack. He soon developed an interest in Bob's theories of gold in the old volcanic crater. Grannis borrowed $500, and the two men formed a partnership. Bob took the money as a grubstake. In return, the dentist was to receive a half interest in anything that was found. The El Paso Lode was a submerged outcrop. Most gold in the district was found between hard layers of igneous rock.

Womack and Grannis induced Professor Henry Lamb of Colorado College to examine their El Paso claim. In his laboratory on campus, Lamb ran assays on the samples he had taken. Some of them tested out at more than $200 to the ton. However, Colorado Springs bankers declined to invest development money, probably because of the discount on Bob's reputation.

Samples of the El Paso's gold ore were placed in the window of Harry Seldomridge's assay office and grain store. Seldomridge arranged a get-together, attended by Grannis, Ed De LaVergne, Professor Lamb and Bob Womack. As a consequence, De LaVergne and Fred Frisbee made an inspection trip up to the El Paso Mine in January. They identified the ore as calaverite, a gold telluride. To celebrate, Bob got drunk again, and was jailed in a cell in City Hall. Colorado Springs' Volunteer Fire Company was located on the floor directly above the lock-up.

Jimmy Doyle and Jimmy Burns were two Irish-American firefighters from Portland, Maine. In spare moments, they listened to Womack's tales of gold in the high basin behind Pikes Peak, and they decided to make a mid-winter visit. During April, a meeting was held at George Carr's cabin. De LaVergne came, as did the Frisbee brothers, Womack and several others. A six-square mile mining district was organized, with George Carr as president. They called it the Cripple Creek Mining District.

Meanwhile, Womack had made the acquaintance of Winfield Scott Stratton, a Colorado Springs carpenter, who would have preferred being a miner. Stratton had lost grubstakes in the Black Hills, at Leadville, in the San Juans and assorted other places. At Womack's urging, Stratton and Billy Fernay made a trip up to Cripple Creek. They pitched their tent below the lower slopes of Battle Mountain. When the tents of others began to go up nearby, Stratton left for home. He returned on July 4, 1891, to stake out a granite ledge that he believed might have been the outer edge of the ancient volcanic crater. Because of the coincidence of the date, he named his claim the Independence.

Another account of how Stratton found the Independence asserts that as he bedded down for the night in his blanket roll, the dying embers from his campfire illuminated the exposed ledge. That night, he dreamed that if he staked a claim on the outcropping, it would make him rich. So vivid was the alleged dream that he decided to act on it, since nothing else had worked. So, without taking time to drink his breakfast, he untethered his mule

FROM THE COLLECTION OF EVELYN AND ROBERT L. BROWN

AFTER CONSIDERABLE development, this view shows Bob Womack's El Paso mine. Unfortunately for him, Womack sold his mine, and he realized only the profits from the sale price.

and hurried down to Colorado City to stake a claim. Before leaving, Stratton filed on a second tract nearby, which he called the Washington. Fearing lawsuits, Stratton did very little work in the daytime, but worked furiously at night. In a short time, he had salted away enough to fight off the inevitable court cases.

As word of these discoveries and rumors of others reached the lower towns, would-be Argonauts, with little or no actual mining experience, packed their wagons with tents and supplies and made their way up Ute Pass. Many came equipped with garden tools, such as hoes and pitchforks, instead of shovels and picks. All over the hillsides adjacent to Womack's log cabin in Poverty Gulch, increasing numbers of new tents appeared.

A. D. Jones and J. K. Miller weretwo druggists from Colorado City. Their business declined as people left for the gold fields. So, they closed up shop and joined the throng headed up the grade to Cripple Creek. Without prior knowledge of mining or how to find a claim, they threw a hat into the air and claimed the spot where it landed. They called it the Pharmacist mine. Its first assay showed some $600 to the ton. Over the years, the Pharmacist produced$500,000 in gold. Cripple Creek was that sort of a place. Traditional mining practices often did not apply at Cripple Creek.

Inevitably, among the earliest arrivals was a Colorado City "madam" who also noted a decline in business. Her name was Blanche Burton. She arrived with a few small tents to shelter a like number of her "girls." She asked for and received advice from Bob Womack concerning the best location for the camp's first brothel. Bob believed that all women, even the "soiled doves," were inherently virtuous. He once fought the patron of a Colorado City saloon who impugned the honor of a bar girl by suggesting that she did "horizontal work." Madam Burton took Bob's advice and set up shop just below the Womack cabin, and began to mine the miners.

Meanwhile, Bob divided his time between giving free advice to newcomers and working his half interest in the El Paso Mine. Finally, he became discouraged and sold his half to Doctor Grannis for $300. Another account, probably apocryphal, relates how he got drunk in a Colorado City saloon and sold his claim for $500. Either way, he lost the El Paso; and, unfortunately, he never found another bonanza. A few years earlier, Bob did sell his Grand View claim for $500 to a man named Edwin Wallace, who later abandoned it.

Bob made his next to last trip up to Cripple Creek in 1902, to attend the Fourth of July celebration. He rode in the parade up Bennett Avenue. His final visit to the town was on July 28, 1904. He made a last nostalgic call at his original cabin. Bob was paralyzed during the last two years of his life. He died at 117 South Limit Street on August 10, 1909, and was laid to rest in Colorado Springs' Evergreen Cemetery.

Although only a few mines were producing gold ore in paying quantities, the word spread rapidly. Nearly a thousand people had already found their way into the basin by 1892.

The rush was on!

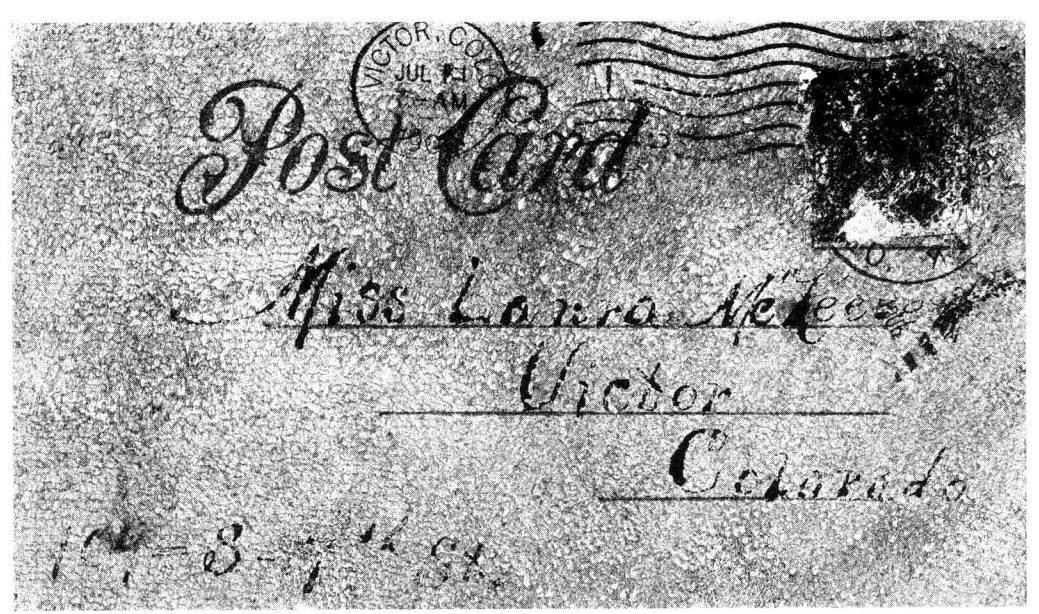

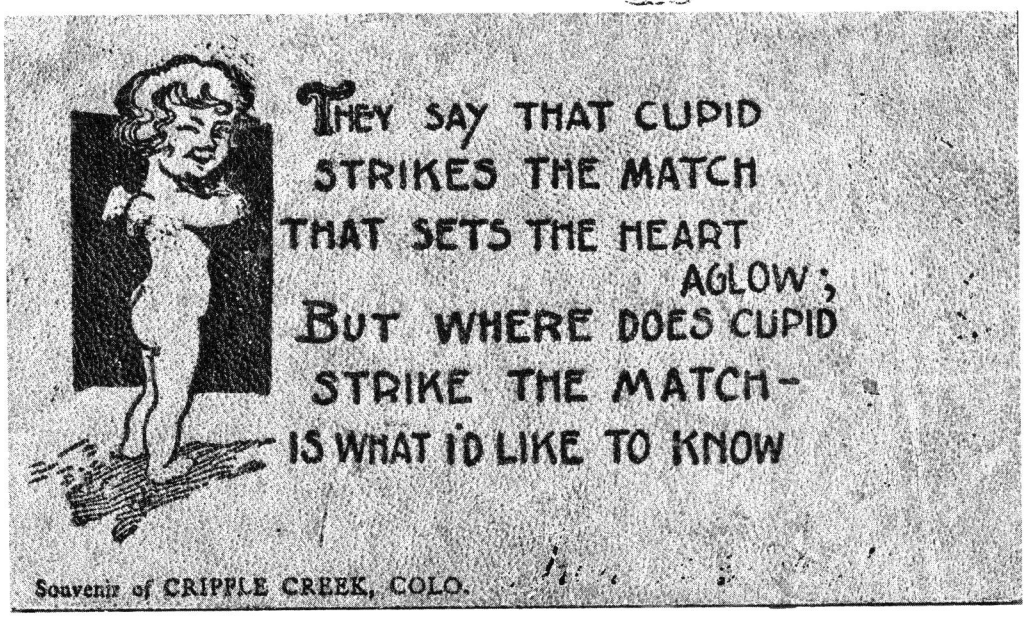

FLIMSY LEATHER POSTCARDS were the bane of postal clerks, but they were popular with the public. This one was mailed from Cripple Creek to Victor in 1906.

COLLECTION OF EVELYN AND ROBERT L. BROWN

FROM THE COLLECTION OF FREDA AND FRANCIS B. RIZZARI

FROM THE WESTERN EDGE of the old crater, here was the original settlement called Fremont, named for the 1842-1855 explorer of Colorado, John C. Fremont.

FROM THE COLLECTION OF FREDA AND FRANCIS B. RIZZARI

A. J. HARLAN, a "scenic photographer" from Barry (Anaconda) — located in the fabulous Cripple Creek Mining District — took this very early view of the original settlement, which was south of the present town of Cripple Creek in 1892.

Hayden Placer, Fremont and Cripple Creek

**VER SINCE** they had purchased it in 1885, a substantial part of the Cripple Creek basin had been the property of the Bennett & Myers Real Estate Company of Denver. George Carr still leased the Broken Box Ranch from this firm. Julius Myers loved to fish the trout streams that flowed down from the edges of the old crater. Horace Bennett disliked the place. When Carr notified the partners that gold had been found on their land and that prospectors were digging holes all over the place, Bennett made a hurry-up trip to Cripple Creek.

At first, Bennett thought that Womack was staging a second Mount Pisgah Hoax. While looking over the place, he discovered that a group of men from Colorado Springs had established a claim to nearly 150 acres near the Broken Box. On April 4, 1891, they registered a claim at the El Paso County Court House. The Springs group had selected the name Hayden Placer, after the well-known leader of the government's 1874 survey, Ferdinand Vandiveer Hayden. Upon further investigation, Bennett decided that Hayden Placer was no more than a thinly-disguised plot to gain possession of government land for establishing a townsite. So, he sent Melvin Sowle, his half brother, up to the "diggings" as a personal observer and reporter.

In order to stay ahead of the Hayden Placer crowd, Bennett authorized Sowle to have the northern part of the Broken Box Ranch surveyed and platted as a townsite. It was to be called Fremont, in honor of the famous pathfinder, John C. Fremont, who led five important expeditions across Colorado between 1842 and 1853. The Fremont townsite was platted on 80 acres during November of 1891. Its streets were named numerically from west to east. Two of those running north and south were named for George Carr and William Eaton. Most of the better homes were on Carr Street. The two principal thoroughfares were called Bennett and Myers avenues. Bennett Avenue was cut across a steep hillside. The south side was 15 feet lower than the north side. To this day, traffic going west takes the upper level, while eastbound cars drive on the lower level.

Most of the finer business houses, hotels, restaurants, apothecary shops, food and hardware stores, as well as the higher-class saloons, were arrayed along Bennett Avenue. However, one block away, Meyers Avenue catered to a different clientele. Julius Myers was a deeply religious man, who taught Sunday school regularly each week until he reached advanced age. He never quite adjusted to the fact that one of the most extensive red-light districts in America had grown up along a street that bore his name. But sometimes in private he laughed about it.

One of the principal organizers of Hayden Placer was Ed DeLaVergne, a pious and moral person who refused to allow saloons, dancehalls or brothels to operate in his town. It became difficult to sell building lots to free and easy miners far away from home and Mary Ann. By contrast, Fremont was a wide-open place. Eventually, the two side by side towns became both awkward and somewhat confusing. Finally, in February of 1893, they merged. With common usage, the always-popular name of Cripple Creek superseded the two previous identities. After all, the new name was more picturesque — and besides, it had the ring of adventure!

Civic improvements were inevitable as new families began to arrive. By 1892, there were an estimated 5,000 people in the new town, and another 5,000 in the surrounding satellite villages. In 1894, the total had jumped to 10,000. Unlike some prior Colorado mining locations, Cripple Creek was always accessible. Since its time occurred late in the 19th century, the town had electric lights, telephone service, telegraph lines and its own water system almost from the beginning. Soon, there were two electric streetcar lines to carry miners to and from their work places. Three railroads ran an estimated 54 trains in and out of the district's two depots each day, bringing in supplies, as well as new people. On their return trips, the trains hauled ore concentrate down to the smelters at Colorado City.

Eight daily or weekly newspapers flourished at one time or another. On Bennett Avenue the Palace and Windsor hotels rented chairs in their lobbies for $1 a night for sleepers, when all the rooms had been rented. Joe Wolfe, a con man who had been run out of Ouray,

FROM THE COLLECTION OF FREDA AND FRANCIS B. RIZZARI

FROM THE WESTERN END of the Cripple Creek Basin, this 1892 view shows the nucleus beginnings, with some of the first buildings along Bennett Avenue. This view was taken by Horace S. Poley.

JAMES A. HARLAN of Colorado Springs and Victor exposed this "Bird's Eye View of Cripple Creek from Globe Hill" in April of 1893. At that time, the town was still quite small.

COLLECTION OF FREDA AND FRANCIS B. RIZZARI

JUDGING BY THE SMALL SIZE of Cripple Creek, this picture was probably made in the early 1890's. It was taken from the southeast, looking toward Mount Pisgah.

arrived and built another hotel. He called it the Continental. Down the street, the National Hotel stood five stories tall. As each stagecoach arrived, the town marshal made it a point to be on hand to confiscate firearms. He sold the guns to pay the salaries of Cripple Creek's teachers. Horace Bennett and railroad tycoon David Moffat opened the Bi-Metallic Bank. Eventually, there were three banks in town, 16 churches, an opera house, stock exchange and 73 saloons.

Between them, the Portland, Anaconda, Mary McKinney, Vindicator and C.O.D. mines were producing a startling $750,000 in gold each month. Remember, too, the price of gold at that time was a scant $20 an ounce. Since some of the best years at Cripple Creek followed on the heels of the Panic of 1893, there was never a shortage of men seeking work in the mines. Unemployed silver miners from Aspen, Leadville, the San Juans and elsewhere were able to find work again at Cripple Creek.

South of Womack's El Paso, John Bernard dug a hole next to a pair of elk antlers on Raven Hill. His Elkton mine produced a whopping $13 million in gold. Billy Davenport came west from Iowa and spent a fortune searching for a paying vein. He located the Doctor Jackpot, which was soon valued at $1,250,000. But of all the fabled mines within the Bowl of Gold, the Cresson probably came the closest to realizing mankind's dream of a veritable nest of the yellow metal. Its location is above the town of Elkton, between Raven and Bull Hill.

The Cresson was the property of Eugene and J. R. Harbeck, who engaged mining engineer Dick Roelofs to sink a 600-foot shaft beside a promising outcropping. He put down a nearly-vertical shaft until in November of 1914, he stopped at a depth of 1,200 feet. There, his excavation opened up a cavern, or vug, that measured 20 x 40 x 15 feet. Its walls were lined with flakes of pure gold crystals in quartz. The prevailing theory holds that the ore had been naturally refined by Nature during the prehistoric volcanic eruption. Over $1,200,000 of this gold was taken out of the mine during the first four weeks alone. A thick vault door was installed at the mine entrance, and three armed guards were always on duty. Each employee was subjected to a thorough daily bodily search and a shower at the end of the work shift to prevent highgrading. Such was the condition of their employment.

Armed guards rode on the top of each railroad car when ore from the Cresson was shipped. One account insists that Cresson shipments by-passed Colorado City's refineries and were sent directly to the mint in Denver. Production to date exceeds $45 million. Dick Roelofs managed the mine for a time, until he embarked upon a well-financed 30 year retirement in New York City.

At its peak, Cripple Creek's population rose to 35,000 persons. It was quite a place.

FROM THE COLLECTION OF EVELYN AND ROBERT L. BROWN

HERE IS A SECOND leather postcard. This one was mailed from Victor to Wymore, Nebraska, in 1906.

FROM THE COLLECTION OF EVELYN AND ROBERT L. BROWN

E. A. YELTON HAD TWO STUDIOS in Cripple Creek. In 1899, he was at 357 Bennett Avenue, and in 1900, he was able to photograph old Cripple Creek before the fire. Mount Pisgah appears at the upper left. Apparently, Yelton had arrived in 1896, as this picture carries the earlier date.

FROM THE SAME ANGLE as the 1896 Yelton photograph, Cripple Creek appears as shown in this contemporary color view at present. Notice the scars of the streets which appeared in the historic Yelton picture.

FROM THE COLLECTION OF EVELYN AND ROBERT L. BROWN

FROM THE COLLECTION OF FRED AND JO MAZZULLA

WINFIELD SCOTT STRATTON was easily the richest and most secretive of the several Cripple Creek millionaires

Winfield Scott Stratton

ENERAL WINFIELD SCOTT was one of the great heroes to emerge from both the War of 1812 and America's War With Mexico. Despite his years, Scott was still the commanding general of Lincoln's Northern Army at the start of the Civil War. It was a common practice during the last century for parents to name children for noted people, hoping that traits of that person would be passed on to the child. Lieutenant Winfield Scott Edgerly and General Winfield Scott Hancock, the noted Indian fighter, were two such examples. So was Winfield Scott Stratton of Jeffersonville, Indiana, who came to Colorado Springs in 1872. He was an excellent carpenter, and soon had a good business going from a shop on Pikes Peak Avenue.

Winfield Scott Stratton would have preferred being a miner, rather than a carpenter. To learn more and to increase his proficiency, he studied assaying with Professor Lamb at Colorado College. Stratton was somewhat of an introvert, albeit a highly intelligent one. Typically, he was moody, suspicious and very fond of whiskey. He trusted few people beyond his shoemaker, Bob Schwartz, the only man who could make boots that did not hurt his feet. He particularly disliked lawyers, stockbrokers and preachers. But at times, he was generous almost to a fault. Among his benefactions were the Colorado School of Mines, Meals for the Homeless, the Salvation Army and Colorado College. He later withdrew the bequest to Colorado College because "colleges breed lawyers."

Stratton preferred his own company to that of others. As noted in a previous chapter, he earned grubstakes by building houses, only to lose them in a variety of Western towns, like Rosita, Granite, Robinson, Kokomo and Red Cliff. He spent 18 months in Leadville only to return home empty-handed.

Stratton tried matrimony only once. In 1876, four years after arriving in Colorado, he married a 17-year-old girl who worked at the boarding house where he lived. Their courtship was brief, only four months. Zeurah Stewart was her name, and she was already pregnant. When she told Stratton, he denied paternity and sent his young spouse packing back to Illinois. Three years after, in 1879, he divorced her. Years later, when Zeurah's son appeared, Stratton wrote a check and sent the boy to the University of Illinois, admonishing him never to return.

Although he never married again, Stratton enjoyed the company of women, but only on his own terms. He was a frequent patron of some the most expensive Myers Avenue parlor houses. Many stories have survived concerning his eccentric behavior. No doubt some of them are true. Others seem to grow more bizarre with each retelling. A few of the most humorous are total fabrications. The following are examples:

In addition to lawyers, stockbrokers and preachers, Stratton mistrusted bankers, and he made regular trips to the teller's window to personally tote up his interest, thereby assuring that he was not being cheated. He nearly always made these pilgrimages on foot. On one particularly cold morning, he observed the rough-and-red hands of local laundry girls, caused by daily exposure to harsh lye soaps. He also noted how the girls were carrying heavy baskets of other peoples' soiled garments from their homes to be laundered. Stratton felt compassion for nearly all unfortunates; and, secretly he made arrangements for new bicycles with luggage carriers to be delivered to the homes of all the laundry girls in the city. Where the bicycles came from became known only after his death.

Although he disliked most members of the clergy and never joined a church, one of his few close associates confided that Father Volpe was unlike most men of the cloth, and that the priest was having a rough time finishing construction of his church. Once again in secret, Stratton put up money to assure completion of the structure. Like the laundresses, Father Volpe discovered the source of the benefaction after Stratton was gone. He also contributed to the Baptists, Presbyterians and to Parson Tom Uzell's skid-row Methodist mission in Denver.

Instead of a mansion in keeping with his wealth, Stratton lived in a modest four-room house at 115 North Weber Street. He disapproved of some of the superficial

FROM THE COLLECTION OF EVELYN AND ROBERT L. BROWN

WINFIELD SCOTT STRATTON'S far-famed Independence mine was sold for the world's record price of $11 million.

IN THIS PRESENT-DAY VIEW of the Independence mine, note the same notch on the hillside above the mine. The adjacent town of Independence grew up to house the workers who labored here.

FROM THE COLLECTION OF EVELYN AND ROBERT L. BROWN

aspects of life in the town, and he referred to Colorado Springs as "Little London," as did others. In truth, the place had become a drawing card for English tourists, capitalists, health-seekers and promoters. Inevitably, some British customs followed the influx. Fox hunting and riding to the hounds were particularly offensive to Stratton since the transplants took to the prairies quite early on Sunday mornings, disturbing his sleep. He often complained of being roused from a sound sleep by "...the ridiculous tootling of English hunting trumpets." Stratton further maintained that in the absence of foxes, the hunters were "...driving the coyotes nuts." He would have loved the description of a later critic who referred to fox hunting as "...the unspeakable in pursuit of the inedible."

Despite negative sentiments expressed about his town, Stratton deeded lots near his home to Colorado Springs, with the provision that a new City Hall should be built there. Since funds were short, he loaned the money to get the construction underway. A new U.S. post office was another Stratton gift, as was an annual $5,000 donation to fund Sunday-afternoon band concerts in Cheyenne Park, which he usually attended, unobtrusively.

When Stratton put up money for the Mining Exchange Building, the local business community tendered a grand banquet in his honor. It was held in the posh Antlers Hotel on January 16, 1902. General William J. Palmer was there, as was ex-governor Adams, the mayor of Colorado Springs and about 65 other dignitaries. Fifteen courses and four varieties of champagne were served. Everyone was present, except the erratic guest of honor, who reportedly stayed at home that evening to share a more modest repast with Bob Schwartz. He noted later that he "...hated tuxedos and refused to wear one," and that he "...had dined out and enjoyed it only once in his life."

One of the most repeated Stratton tales concerns how he allegedly came into possession of Denver's Brown Palace Hotel. There are many versions. As noted elsewhere, Stratton was fond of all women, especially the fallen ones. Some who knew him have maintained that he kept a "favorite" in every first-class hotel, in each of the several towns within the Cripple Creek district. When a girl pleased him, she could look forward to a weekend at the Brown Palace with Stratton, but under an assumed name. Late in the evening on one such sojourn, he ordered that a case of champagne be sent up to his room. For the next several minutes he amused himself by dropping bottles off the balcony into the lobby below. Predictably, the manager sent up the hotel bouncer to eject "John Smith," and his little friend. Infuriated, Stratton roused Henry C. Brown at 2:00 A.M., wrote a check for $1 million, bought the hotel, and proceeded to fire the bouncer and the manager. Armed with a second case of champagne, he returned to the balcony and resumed dropping bottles into the lobby.

In another version of the same tale, Stratton became incensed when he tried to register with Madam Lola Livingston of the Old Homestead Parlor House. When the manager refused, Stratton went to Brown, purchased the hotel and fired the clerk so that he and Lola could spend the weekend in either the Presidential or the Bridal suites — accounts vary. Real-estate man, Horace Bennett, loved this yarn, and often repeated variations of it.

Although colorful and possibly in character with what the unpredictable Stratton might have done, if it had occurred to him, the Brown Palace narratives are untrue. Stratton never owned the Brown Palace. But when Henry Brown was well up in years, he became a victim of hard times, and was about to lose everything. He appealed to Stratton for help in avoiding foreclosure. Stratton purchased a mortgage from Equitable Life for $650,000 to save the hotel and Brown's estate. Some years after the death of both men, Brown's heirs regained possession of the hotel.

Very few men ever dared to invade Stratton's domain where his women were concerned. Jimmy Burns once took a Stratton "favorite" to a Victor hotel, where he bribed the manager to bolt all outside doors. When Stratton discovered the perfidy, he bought the hotel, got the keys and kicked Burns and the girl into the street. Spontaneous purchases of hotels were common features in these yarns.

Following the 1893 silver crash, Stratton gave $85,000 through the Salvation Army to feed destitute miners. That same year, he wrote a $15,000 check to H.A.W. Tabor to save him from poverty. It was mailed to Baby Doe with a note admonishing her not to tell Tabor. It was found in her effects and is in the Colorado Historical Society's Tabor Collection. It was Stratton who built the vault in Tabor's Leadville bank. Tabor once asked Stratton for a loan. Stratton tore up his I.O.U. as soon as the old man was out the door. He also bailed out Tabor's widow by paying off the assessments against the worthless Matchless mine, located above Leadville, where Baby Doe died during the winter of 1935. It was Stratton who gave several thousand dollars to the destitute Womack during those last few years, virtually the only Colorado mining baron who remembered the contributions of "Crazy Bob."

For many years, Cripple Creek's "Midas" held down production of his Independence property to a mere $2,000 each month, just enough to meet his expenses. Later, as his empire expanded, he allowed $1 million in gold to be extracted annually.

While his enormous wealth had come from the mining of gold, Stratton supported William Jennings Bryan for the presidency because he thought Bryan's free-silver policies would be best for Colorado's people. Once he offered to bet that Bryan would win. Unfortunately, Bryan lost three times, in 1896, 1900 and in 1908. The "Barefoot Boy Orator of the Platte" had advocated coinage of 16 ounces of silver to one ounce of gold. "Sixteen to One" became his campaign slogan. Fortunately, nobody ever offered to cover Stratton's bet on Bryan.

From time to time, various people approached Stratton to find out if he would consider selling the Independence Mine. Time after time, he steadfastly refused even to discuss it. It has been conservatively estimated that by 1898, he had already taken more than $4 million from the Independence, despite the limits he had imposed on removal of the ore.

It was a shrewd 35 year old Denver financier who finally got W. S. Stratton to begin negotiations, although outwardly he still declined to sell his mine. However, Verner Reed had his foot in the door, and that was a start. Benjamin Franklin once said, "Neither a fortress nor a virgin will hold out for long after they begin to negotiate."

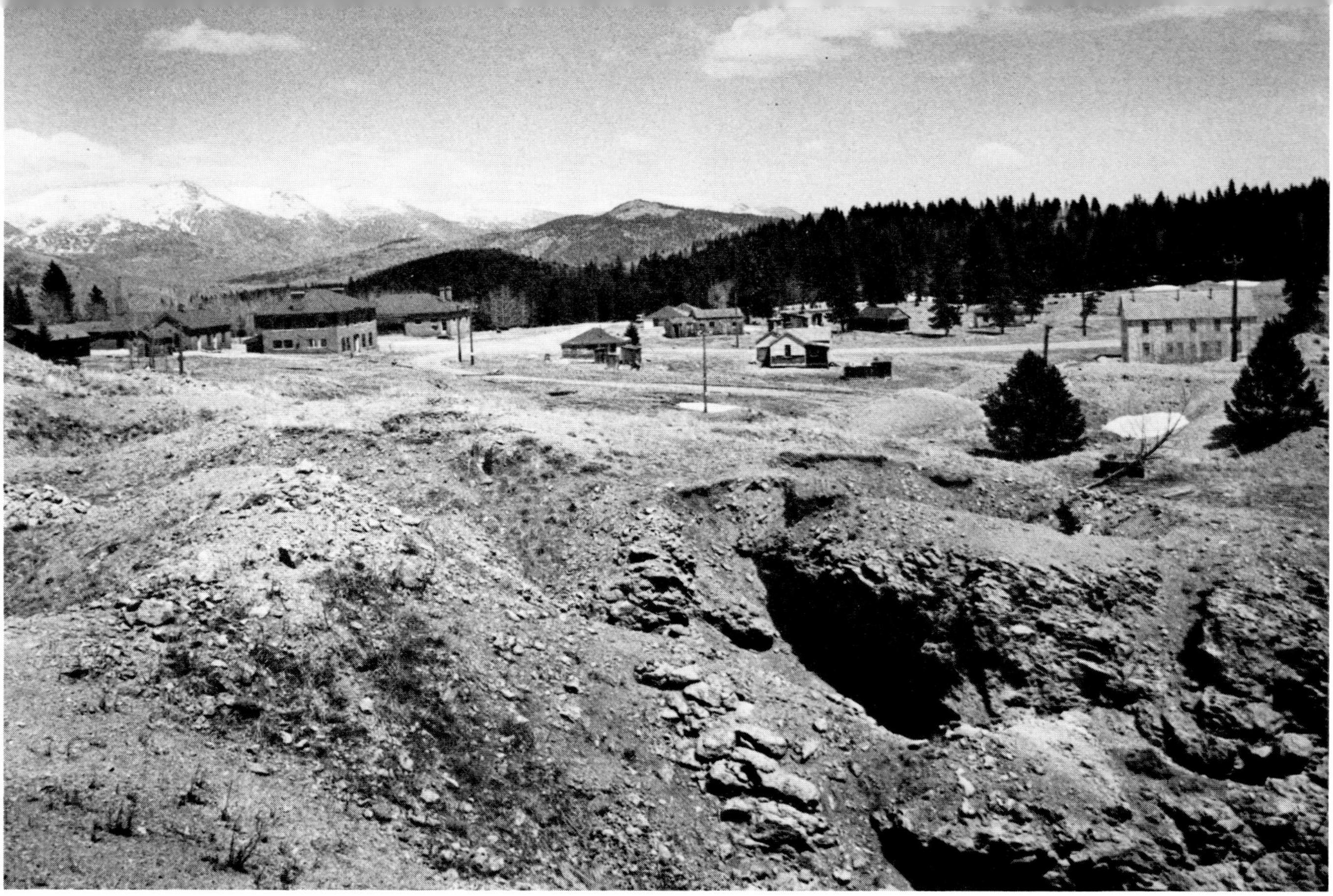

ON THE TOP OF GLOBE HILL, directly above Cripple Creek, Winfield Scott Stratton established the settlement of Winfield as a headquarters for his many ac-

AT WINFIELD, the brick structure at far left housed Stratton's records. The large two-story barracks was for unmarried men who worked for the "Midas of the Rockies"

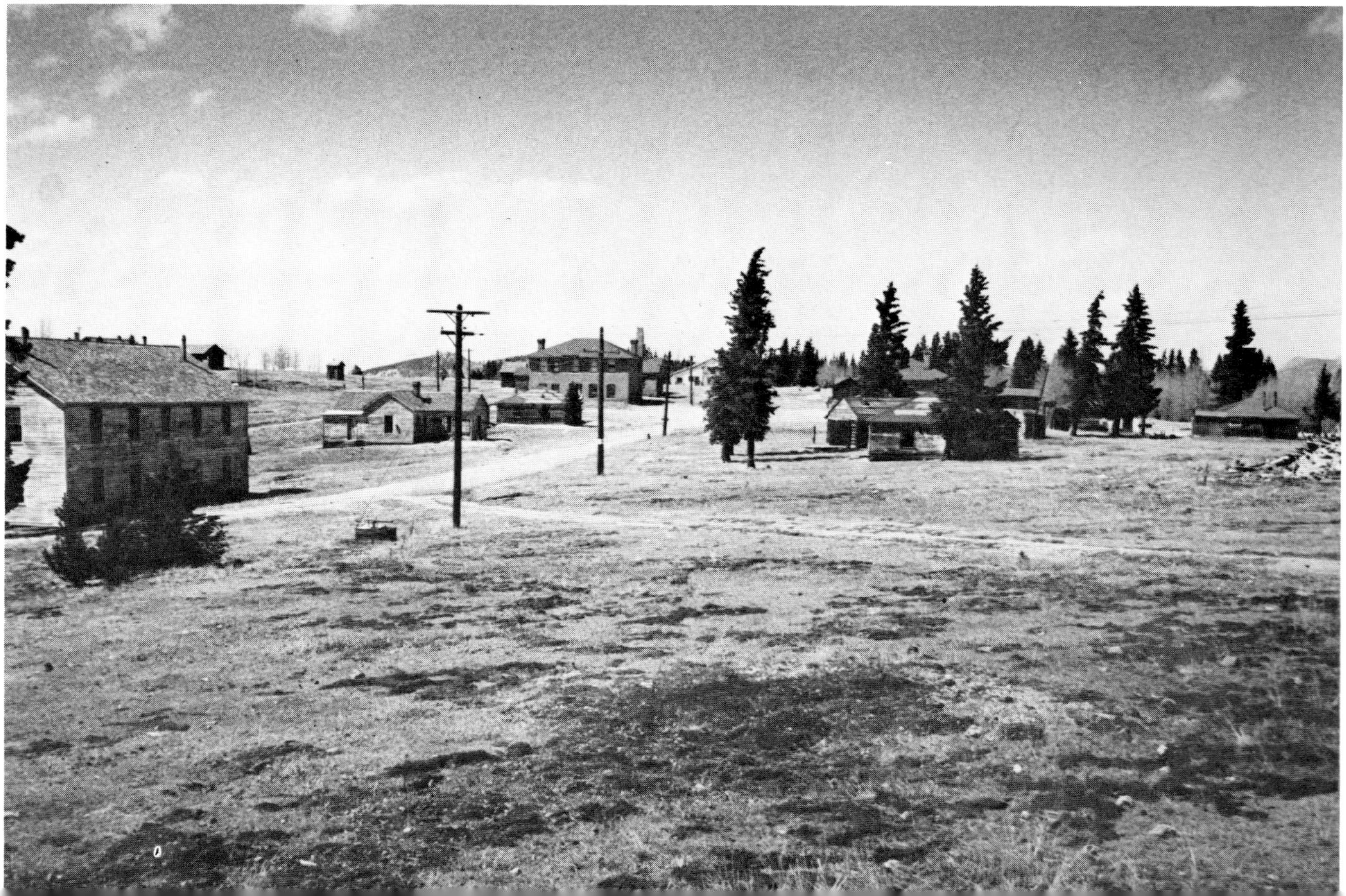

Reed acted as a go-between for the British Venture Corporation and Winfield Stratton. A new English corporation, called Stratton's Independence, Limited, was formed in 1899. A record price of $11 million was agreed upon. Verner Reed took a commission of $1 million, while Stratton, now in England, received $10 million for his mine. The contract was signed on April 27, 1899.

Back in Colorado once more, Stratton's always fragile health began to deteriorate. For the next two years, his appetite for solid food declined, while his craving for whiskey increased. Although he had been a diabetic for many years, he now consumed a quart of whiskey daily. He became even more of a recluse now, except for a fairly steady parade of women of questionable character, who were observed entering and leaving the little house on North Weber. Although he never sought to conceal public knowledge of these nocturnal visitations, he became very secretive about a wonderful new project, which would occupy his energies during his last years.

Once he had worked through the details in his own mind, Stratton called reporters and mining men to his office in June of 1901. There, he announced a few of the particulars of his so-called Umbrella, Wine Glass or "Bowl of Gold" theory. He reasoned that the Cripple Creek Basin was crossed with many rich veins of gold ore, which tended to converge, like the arms of an umbrella, toward a common center, or mother vein, the throat or vortex of the ancient volcano. By his calculations, the vortex would be below Iron Clad Hill, near the town of Midway. It could possibly be below the Plymouth Rock mine, although *The Pueblo Chieftain* placed the source under Globe or Gold hills. Later, Stratton decided that those two hills would be closer to the center point he sought.

During the previous two years, Stratton had studied the mines and maps of the mining district carefully, and had watched as claims came up for sale, acquiring those that he felt might be needed. Finally, he owned all of the desired property, about one-fifth of the actual mining area. His plan was to sink a 3,500-foot vertical shaft. Its estimated cost would be $8 million. He expected to strike a nest of pure gold at about the level of the plains.

Redwood timbers of near-record size were imported from California. As work progressed, it became necessary to drill horizontal tunnels in order to drain off the underground water before deeper drilling could continue. Each time the water table was drained, there was a corresponding lowering of water levels in other mines of the district. In most cases, even deeper deposits of gold were revealed.

Late in the summer of 1902, Stratton became ill again. This time, he took to his bed and remained there for a month. At this point, a priest, Father Bender, had become a confidant, the only man of the cloth that Stratton could, or would, tolerate. Father Bender came often to pray at the bedside. Stratton's death occurred at 9:35 A.M. on September 10, 1902. He was just 54 years of age. His demise was caused by hypertrophic cirrhosis of the liver, with diabetic complications. His body lay in state in the Mining Exchange Building, with a guard of honor. Burial was in Evergreen Cemetery.

Stratton's death caused his "Bowl of Gold" theory to collapse. Since 1902, no person or syndicate has cared enough to gamble on the wily Stratton's conjecture. Anyway, the few parties who did show an interest, lacked the financing for such a gamble. Probably, we shall never know if his theory had any validity or not.

Stratton's will bequeathed various sums to an assortment of institutions, friends and a few relatives. Isaac Stratton, Zeurah's son, got $350,000, which he lost in California real-estate schemes. After that, he became a bank clerk. The remainder of the W. S. Stratton estate was placed in trust to pay for a home for needy senior citizens and dependent children. This was the Myron Stratton Home, named for his father. Its doors opened in November of 1909. It still operates at the south edge of Colorado Springs, on the east side of Colorado Highway 115. To date, it has cared for over 1,000 persons.

The city of Colorado Springs had hoped, instead, for a parks system, a sanatorium, a hospital, or for a public library. Instead, he gave "Little London" a home for paupers. Even *The Denver Post* editorialized against "the poorhouse."

Stratton's well-known hatred of attorneys followed him to the grave. He once said that if he had $10 million, he would cheerfully spend all of it putting every lawyer in Colorado behind bars. Now, the lawyers descended on his estate with nearly 15 years of litigation. There were a variety of lawsuits, including one from a phony sister, many "true partners," and at least a dozen secret wives and abandoned widows.

Quiet, moody, reserved Winfield Scott Stratton was gone, but his beloved Cripple Creek continued to produce incredible quantities of gold.

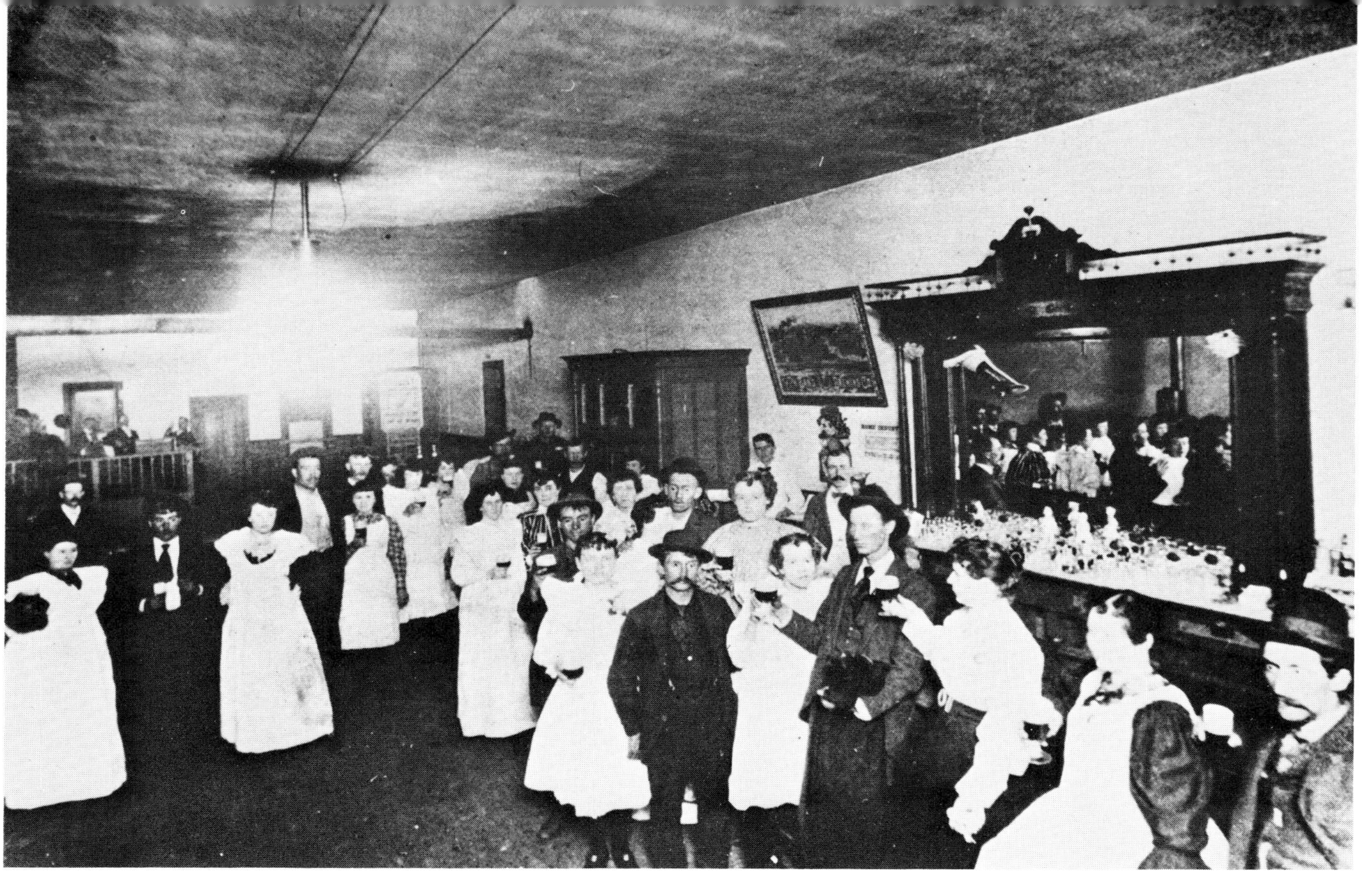

NOTORIOUS MYERS AVENUE was the address of the rowdy Crapper Jack's Saloon. Notice the eyes on the man at lower right, the orchestra at far left and several "hostesses."

THE KILDAY & WELD White House Saloon was one of Cripple Creek's most popular. Notice the preponderance of mustaches, the sheriff's gun belt and "our pet" at far right.

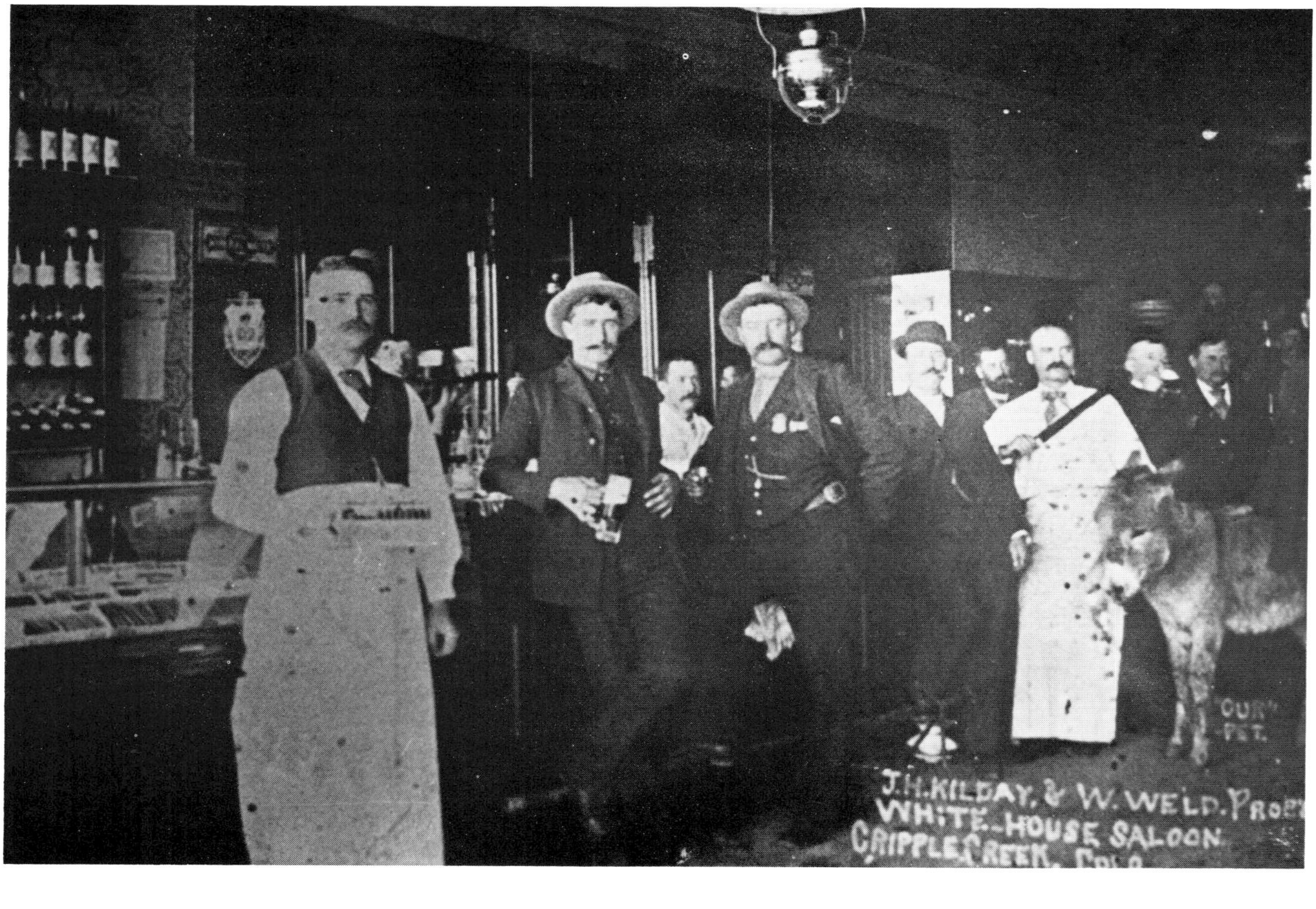

Life Among the Miners

T HAD BEEN A STRUGGLE just getting to Colorado's earlier gold and silver-mining locations. Crossing Kansas or Nebraska in canvas-topped wagons during the summer was no picnic. But economic hard times caused people to throw caution to the four winds. Each year, far too many expired of cholera, diarrhea and other diseases. Although spring promised warmer weather, wagon trains often were detained until the Iowa mud had dried up. Fall was a nice time, too, but prairie fires ignited by electrical storms were a constant peril after the wild grass had dried. Also, there was the possibility of unseasonal snowstorms, which could roar across the Great Plains anytime after the end of August. Then, too, Westerners' memories still retained vivid images of the 1846–'47 fate of the Donner Party's ordeal in the snow.

Cripple Creek was not only the greatest of Colorado's rushes, it was the last one, as well. Since it occurred at a much later time, getting there had become infinitely easier. America's first transcontinental railroad, the Union Pacific, finally had been completed in 1869, connecting the East with the Pacific Coast, as the corporate name implies. The Santa Fe, Northern Pacific, Great Northern, Rio Grande, Southern Pacific and other Western lines had already criss-crossed the American West well before the 1890's, and ticket costs were comparatively modest. A pioneer headed for Cripple Creek could ride a succession of trains all the way to Denver and Colorado Springs. Several daily stagecoach lines scheduled runs between the Springs and Cripple Creek. Beginning in 1894, people could finally ride a train all the way up to Cripple Creek itself on the narrow-gauge Florence & Cripple Creek Railroad.

Once they had reached their destination, they found that life was still harsh for the average person, especially during the opening years. Upon arriving, they found the hotels and boarding houses were overcrowded. They slept in chairs or on tables in restaurants, or on the floors of saloons. Most people lived in tents, if they had them.

Early photographs show large numbers of white-canvas tents scattered throughout the basin. Even though trees were somewhat sparse at this elevation, log cabins soon replaced the tents, especially after a prolonged cold spell. settlers. Soon, there were eight lumber yards, all doing good businesses. For those individuals who chose not to build, it was possible to rent one or two-room shacks, with vertical batten-board siding, for $15 a month; or they could be purchased outright for $500. Inside, the walls were lined with

FROM THE COLLECTION OF EVELYN AND ROBERT L. BROWN

'MADAM' PEARL DeVERE'S final resting place is marked by a heart-shaped stone in Cripple Creek's Mount Pisgah cemetery, the headstone has been stolen some time after this picture was taken.

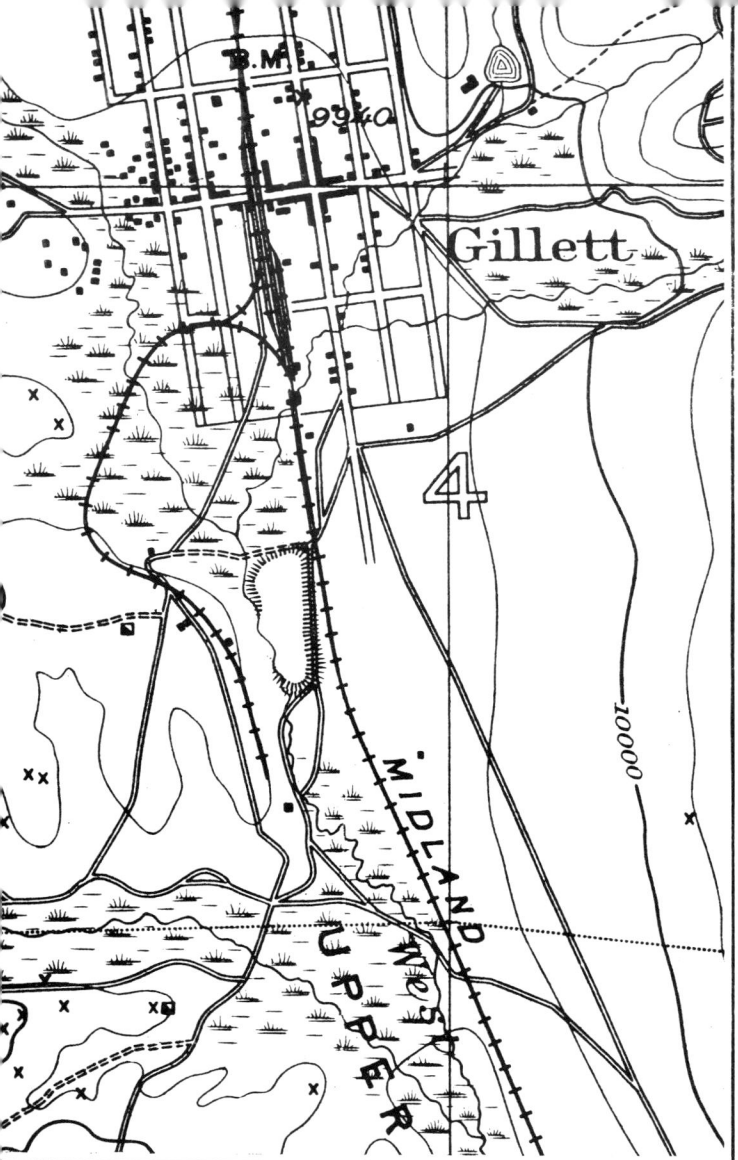

ON AUGUST 24, 1894, J. G. Wilson exposed this picture of Gillett's race track at the time of the bull fight.

FROM THE COLLECTION OF EVELYN AND ROBERT L. BROWN

FROM THE COLLECTION OF FRED AND JO MAZZULA

GILLETT'S RACE TRACK was the scene of the only genuine Mexican bull fight ever held in the U.S.A. Arizona Charlie Meadows is on the white horse at right.

FROM THE COLLECTION OF EVELYN AND ROBERT L. BROWN

DETECTIVE CARL MATTHEWS of the Colorado Springs police department allowed us to copy his Gillett bull-fight ticket.

FROM THE COLLECTION OF FREDA AND FRANCIS B. RIZZARI

BARELY OUTSIDE THE RIM of the old crater was the location of the town of Gillett. Father Volpe's church dominates the foreground.

newspapers, while the ceilings were often covered with canvas. Kerosene (coal-oil) lamps provided illumination and coal- or wood-burning stoves were used for heat. Florence, south of Cripple Creek, was the nearest source for cheap coal.

A majority of those who came to Cripple Creek brought some sort of religious beliefs. Several churches flourished almost from the beginning. The first was a Congregational church, although approximately a third of the total population was Roman Catholic. In an openly bigoted way, Asians and persons of southern European stock were discouraged from taking up residence.

Since drinking establishments were expected to close on the Sabbath, the first regular Sunday school met in Goldfield's Buckhorn Saloon. Buxom, trumpet-voiced Mother Duffy owned the place. When the preacher arrived, she would order "the girls" down from the upstairs rooms to constitute a choir. One morning, a drunk interrupted the "pulpit pounder" and noisily demanded to be served at the bar. Mother Duffy seized him by the scruff of the neck and the seat of the pants. Her voice modulated into the dulcet whine of a middle-aged airedale. Then, with a few well-chosen words from the Scriptures, she hurled him bodily into the manure-laden street.

Including the Buckhorn, there were already 26 saloons in the mining district by 1893. Following the silver crash, many out-of-work miners moved up to Cripple Creek, and the number of saloons shot up to 73 by the end of that same year. They sported names like the Opera Club, Miners' Exchange, Old Yellowstone, Newport, Dawson Club, Swanee River, Palace, Linwood Club and the inevitable Last Chance. Other thirst-quenchers were identified only by the names of such owners as Harvey Moulton, Marius Durand, the Swackenberg Brothers, and Will S. Wood. Most of them sold beers for a nickel and offered free lunches, which were free for paying customers only. To facilitate cleaning, sawdust-covered floors were common, and were changed on Sundays. Sam Altman's sawmill had standing orders for sawdust to be delivered on Sunday mornings to the local drinking establishments.

Some saloons were also dancehalls, like Crapper Jack's on Myers Avenue. Several called themselves variety theaters. They had small stages at the end of the rooms, where little orchestras played during productions by traveling shows that moved from town to town each week. Bare-knuckle boxing matches, as well as bull versus bear fights took up any slack time between shows.

Perusal of state business directories from the 1890's reveal that eight newspapers were published in the district. Reading rooms, social clubs and schools could usually be found in the larger towns. Also listed were bath houses, 24 grocery stores and nine assay offices. The degree of "high-grading" can usually be estimated by the number of assayers in a town. Using the "five-fingered discount," miners squirreled out rich ore samples in their lunch buckets or hidden on their persons. Most assayers functioned as so-called "fences." The pick-up points were usually in the saloons. In some of the towns, it was common to find raw ore in church collection plates. Merchants encouraged high-grading as a stimulus to business. If caught and taken to court, miners' juries were reluctant to convict since everybody did it.

Directories also show ten barber shops, one very busy undertaker, and despite Mr. Stratton's preferences, 44 lawyers. Wesley Gourley's Anheuser Busch was the first hotel. It opened in 1891. Joe Wolfe's Continental had sleeping rooms for 200 people. Then, in 1892, the posh Clarendon opened its doors. Following the 1896 fires, the brick Imperial Hotel was constructed. Today, it is the only one of the original hostelries still standing and in operation. All of its rooms are furnished with 1890's furniture. During the summer months, the Imperial has a superb melodrama theater, which plays twice daily, except Mondays, in the Gold Bar Room Theatre. Meals are served amid Victorian decor in the main-floor dining room.

Since Cripple Creek boomed during the 1890's, there were many civic improvements available. Two electric interurban lines, a High Line and a Low Line, carried miners to and from their work. The fare was just five cents. Between them, the two lines ran cars every half

FROM THE COLLECTION OF EVELYN AND ROBERT L. BROWN

INSIDE THE OLD HOMESTEAD the original furnishings and decor have been faithfully preserved. The brass-eagle card holder on the door once contained the girl's "professional" name.

hour. The High Line was the highest interurban route in North America. At its highest point, the electric cars reached 10,487 feet in elevation near Midway on Bull Hill. The interurban lines' 12 miles of track extended all the way between Cripple Creek and Victor. The Low Line served Elkton and Anaconda. Since both electric lines were owned by the Colorado Springs & Cripple Creek District Railway, commonly called the "Short Line", they were able to use that railroad's trackage. Each car could carry 40 seated passengers, but often carried more as "standees." Regular stops were made at the largest mines. After the interurban service was abandoned in 1920, the Low Line was converted to a road.

Electricity was available for homes and businesses, while arc lights illuminated the principal streets in Cripple Creek. Electricity also lighted most of the district's deep shafts, making miner's candle lights a thing of the past. Some traditions are slow to die. Until ordinances were passed a decade or so ago, pet burros ran free in the town. The burros are still there, but they are now kept in fenced yards!

Throughout U.S. history, whenever a significat but unexpected event occurred, such as the discovery of a new oil field, a war or a major ore discovery, a shift in population seemed to follow. The initial transmigration to Cripple Creek involved many young and unattached males. Equally inevitable has been the nearly simultaneous arrival of an assortment of parasites, who come to care for and exploit the alleged needs of lonely young men who find themselves far from home and "the girls they left behind." These hangers-on include gamblers, criminals, con men, saloon keepers and hard-eyed harlots. Usually, they congregate and share common ground, as close as possible to the center of the activity that originally attracted them.

Just a block down the hill from the respectable Bennett Avenue, and paralleling it, was Myers Avenue, named for the pious Julius Myers. As noted in a previous chapter, while Bennett Avenue became the location of the better restaurants, hotels and the nicer retail shops, Myers became what has been estimated to have been America's biggest and longest honky-tonk district. There were several blocks of gambling houses, saloons, cribs and parlor houses, such as the Trilby and the Old Homestead.

In Chapter 5, there is a brief mention of Blanche Burton, whose early arrival accords her clear title as Cripple Creek's first "madam." Where she came from originally remains a mystery. Nobody is sure that Blanche Burton was her real name, since most of the "women of the half world" adopted aliases. Some who knew her maintained that she had come of a good family and that she had a daughter in a convent. After operating a brothel in Cripple Creek for many years, she retired to live in Colorado City sometime after the turn of the century.

Mrs. Burton was a perfect example of the madam with a heart of gold, a much-cherished stereotype. While living in Colorado City, she purchased many tons of coal for poor families and performed many other charitable acts. On December 21, 1909, an oil lamp exploded, scattering burning oil over her clothing. She died of the burns that same day. Mrs. Burton was only 50 years old at the time of her death. She was interred at Fairview Cemetery in Colorado City, where her grave remained unmarked for seven decades. The late Bill Henderson, banker, his-

FROM THE COLLECTION OF FREDA AND FRANCIS B. RIZZARI

CARR AVENUE, a block from Bennett, is the location of this W. E. Hook picture. Hook's studio operated in Manitou Springs and Colorado Springs between 1888 and 1897.

FROM THE SAME ANGLE as the Hook picture, here is Carr Avenue in 1990. Bennett Avenue is visible to the right in both pictures.

FROM THE COLLECTION OF EVELYN AND ROBERT L. BROWN

FROM THE COLLECTION OF EVELYN AND ROBERT L. BROWN

BENNETT AVENUE was built across a hillside, necessitating that westbound traffic take the upper level, while eastbound vehicles used the lower part of the street. In this view, we see a Fourth of July parade going eastbound, while spectators occupy the retaining wall.

THIS VIEW shows the same split-level of Bennett Avenue, with several of the same structures in the background.

FROM THE COLLECTION OF EVELYN AND ROBERT L. BROWN

FROM THE COLLECTION OF EVELYN AND ROBERT L. BROWN

CRIPPLE CREEK was always "big" on celebrations of any sort. In this instance, it is a Fourth of July parade up Bennett Avenue in 1895. The view looks east.

IN THIS CONTEMPORARY VIEW, we see Bennett Avenue from the same angle shown in the Fourth of July parade picture.

FROM THE COLLECTION OF EVELYN AND ROBERT L. BROWN

torian and former Colorado Springs mayor, was instrumental in placing a grave marker in 1983.

Some 250 to 300 "ladies of the night" worked on Myers Avenue, between 3rd and 5th streets, at the peak of the boom. East of 3rd Street, Myers Avenue was called Poverty Gulch. It extended up the hill, well beyond the Midland Terminal Railroad depot. Here, the aesthetically inclined patron could find the cribs of the "freelance" girls, where Japanese, Mexican, Indian, Spanish, Chinese, French and Negro prostitutes plied their trade. The price decreased as one walked further up the gulch. Most of the cribs were two-room shacks, with the girl's name on the door instead of a house number. The rear room was usually a small kitchen, with a wood or coal burning range. All solicitation was accomplished from the front doorway. By city ordinance, the window shades were closed at all times. A close friend of the writer once confided that as a youth growing up in Cripple Creek, he earned pocket money by delivering 25 cent bundles of firewood to the cribs each night. He also started the fires in the pot-bellied stoves. If the girl was "busy," the 25 cents was always on the top of the chest of drawers.

City fathers exacted a "tax" of $6 each month for each girl and $16 for each madam. Periodic physical ex-

FROM THE COLLECTION OF EVELYN AND ROBERT L. BROWN

HERE, WE ARE LOOKING EAST along Bennett Avenue. Notice that the Midland Terminal depot had not appeared as yet at the end of the street. The Palace Hotel, where Sam Strong was killed, shows on the left, in the middle distance. Notice also the 25¢ and 50¢ rates at the Mt. Pisgah House at the extreme right.

THIS COLOR PICTURE looks east on Bennett Avenue. Although the Mt. Pisgah House and the Palace Hotel are gone, the Midland Terminal depot shows at the end of the street. The Midland Terminal depot now houses the District Museum.

FROM THE COLLECTION OF EVELYN AND ROBERT L. BROWN

aminations kept the incidence of disease low. Deaths from overdoses of morphine, laudinum and chloroform were not uncommon. One frail sister, severely depressed did it the hard way with carbolic acid.

By 1893, there were already 11 brothels in operation, and new ones sprang up each month. At times, their names were suggestive, but not always. There were The Mikado, The Library, Great View, The Boston, Ironclad, The Parisian, Old Faithful, Red Onion, Bon Ton, Casino, Topic, Red Light and Crapper Jack's. Some of the madams were Minnie Smith, Hazel Vernon, Mollie King, Laura Bell, Lollie Lee and the beautiful Pearl De Vere, manager of the posh Old Homestead, at 353 Myers, a favorite of Winfield Scott Stratton.

Most of these establishments were open around the clock. Myers Avenue was 433 yards long. Demand for those services offered there was such that one of the trolley lines found it profitable to lay tracks along the street. This "tenderloin" proved to be a magnet for traveling clergy, who preached on street corners. Even Carry Nation came. She rode the Midland line up from Colorado Springs during August of 1906, after provoking a riot in Denver. There is an account, probably apocryphal, that a delegation from Myers Avenue's saloons met her at the train with money-filled hats in hand. The cash could be hers, they implored, if she would just get back on that train and leave Cripple Creek alone. Allegedly, she accepted, and the town was spared.

A good friend, whose parents and grandparents lived in Cripple Creek around the turn of the century, recalled how the "girls of the line" would exit the back doors of their establishments and walk over to Bennett Avenue for their lunches during the noon lull. Then, at about 2:30 or 3:00 P.M., when the restaurant business quieted down, a parade of businessmen would slip out from their rear doors, cross over to Myers Avenue to "collect" for those lunches, a unique sort of "exchange of services."

Sometimes, there would be early evening parades, as the crib girls dressed in their finery to be driven in coaches up and down Bennett Avenue. Most of the red-light houses were on the north side of Myers Avenue, while the saloons and gambling dens were across the street. A few opium dens were located in an alley behind Myers, where those who were so inclined, could partake of a siege at the poppy pipes.

The original Old Homestead was managed by Hazel Vernon. It was of wooden-frame construction, and was destroyed in the great fire of April, 1896. But the Old Homestead rose from its ashes and was rebuilt as a two-story brick structure. It had maids, a porter, musicians, telephones and a butler. All of its rooms were heated by charcoal stoves. Today, it is operated as a museum of the world's oldest profession. On the ground floor, one may view the parlor, dining room, kitchen and a small bar. At the top of the stairs, a "viewing room" allowed wealthy patrons to choose among the five resident girls as they entered and disrobed. Their rooms along the short hall still contain original furnishings. A brass card holder on each door revealed the "trade name" of the occupant.

Best known of the madams of the Old Homestead was beauteous Pearl De Vere. Her flame-red hair, smooth complexion and costly wardrobe set her apart from others of her calling. During the course of a fancy party in June of 1897, Pearl excused herself, complaining of not feeling well. Later, she was found in her room, fully clothed, after having ingested an overdose of morphine. A sister arrived from the East to claim the body, but when she discovered the nature of Pearl's profession, she disowned Pearl, refused to accept the corpse and returned home.

In spite of this rebuff, the town was equal to the occasion, especially for one of its own. Following a grand funeral, a procession escorted the casket through Bennett Avenue and on to the Mount Pisgah Cemetery. There were four mounted policemen, floral wreaths from as far away as Denver, and a contingent of several hundred men who walked behind the hearse. Their wives and other proper ladies watched the parade from behind closed lace curtains to see who was in the line of march. A 20-piece band from the Elks Club led the mourners, while softly playing the Death March. At the very end of the parade, a number of closed black buggies carried heavily veiled "painted ladies" from the row.

As Pearl's coffin was lowered into the ground, Joe Moore lifted his silver cornet to his lips and played the doleful strains of "Good Bye Little Girl, Good Bye." On the return to town, Moore and the band burst forth with a sprightly rendition of "There'll Be a Hot Time in the Old Town Tonight!"

One of the most hilarious of the true stories of Myers Avenue occurred in March of 1914, when **Colliers Weekly Magazine** sent one of its best known writers out to do a feature story about Colorado. His name was Julian Street, and he was just 34 years old. In Colorado Springs he took a room at the Antlers Hotel. During his stay he met Spencer Penrose, who not only regaled hime with glowing accounts of Cripple Creek, but made available a private railroad car, with a butler, to take Street up on the scenic "Short Line." Colorado's weather in April can be uncertain. It had been a lovely, sunny day when the train pulled out of Colorado Springs. But snow was falling when it pulled into the depot at Cripple Creek. The train was late, a reception committee had met the wrong train, and the noted scribe had only an hour before he must return.

It was cold, and Julian was not dressed for it. In the snowstorm he missed Bennett Avenue and wandered up Myers. At Fourth and Myers a woman invited him into her little house to warm himself by her stove. Street accepted. His benefactor was Madam Leo, who once stood in the center of the street, intoxicated, howling, "I'm Leo the lion." Her bright red hair stood out from her head like a lion's mane, defying brush or comb. Street soon figured out what he had wandered into, excused himself and started walking back toward the depot. As he passed other cribs, he was accorded several other invitations before reaching the safety of his private railroad car.

The long-awaited article appeared in the November, 1914, issue of **Colliers**. Street praised Colorado Springs and the Short Line railroad, but when he got around to Cripple Creek, he wrote some unfortunate and unflattering observations about the city, solely on the basis of what he had seen and experienced in that single hour. Understandably, Cripple Creek was incensed, and even the churches protested. The City Council convened a special meeting. After a heated discussion, a vote to sue **Colliers** was approved, unless the magazine printed an apology or a retraction. **Colliers** replied that Julian Street was a reputable journalist, and that they would stand by his article.

The council met at the Elks Club the second time.

FROM THE COLLECTION OF EVELYN AND ROBERT L. BROWN

GOLDFIELD WAS A FAMILY TOWN, proud of having the longest operating Sunday school in the Cripple Creek district. The distinctive Town Hall had not been built at the time this picture was made.

FROM THE SAME vantage point, this view shows the contemporary gold-mining town of Goldfield — complete with the historic Town Hall.

FROM THE COLLECTION OF EVELYN AND ROBERT L. BROWN

FROM THE COLLECTION OF FREDA AND FRANCIS B. RIZZARI

THE TITLE OF THIS PICTURE is "Fremont, 1891." Comparison with the picture of Womack's cabin reveals that it is the same structure. The man in the doorway is unidentified.

Over in a corner someone spoke, and those within earshot burst forth in gales of laughter. Loud chuckles spread around the hall. At last, a member of the council stood and introduced a formal motion that the name of Myers Avenue be changed to Julian Street. It was done, but for some reason, today's street signs proclaim the street as Myers Avenue once more. For the reader who wishes to read Julian Street's essay in its entirety, the book *Colorado*, by W. Storrs Lee, has reproduced it. Myers Avenue continued to operate until the last crib closed its doors in 1914, not long after the *Colliers* piece appeared.

Joe Wolfe was a con man who had been chased out of Oklahoma. They ran him out of Ouray, too. For a time, he worked as a "tourist gypper" in Manitou Springs. Shortly after his arrival in Cripple Creek, he built the multi-storied Continental Hotel. However, he is remembered today for a totally different enterprise. One day in 1895, he read in a newspaper that the Secretary of Agriculture wanted to lower the price of beef by permitting free entry of cattle from Mexico. Wolfe reasoned that if cows could be brought in, why not bulls?

So, Wolfe entered into a loose partnership with a like-minded seven-foot-tall rodeo performer named Arizona Charlie Meadows. They formed the Joe Wolfe Grand National Spanish Bull Fight Company. Charles Tutt and Spencer Penrose owned a race track at the town of Gillett. Wolfe figured that it might be adapted to a bull fight arena. They made arrangements in Mexico for several fighting bulls and an assortment of *matadors*, *picadors* and other appropriate personnel to accompany the animals. A decision was made to stage the event on August 24, 25 and 26, 1895.

In the meantime, Francis Hill, secretary of the Colorado Humane Society, got word of the scheme and secured a court injunction, detaining the bulls at the Texas border. As the dates approached, Wolfe and Meadows were desperate. So, they went down to the ranches in Phantom Canyon and purchased seven farm bulls. Since these animals had never been abused or tortured, there was little fight in them. In the meantime, Señor José Marrero and his cortege arrived on schedule. To assure financial success, Jefferson Randolph "Soapy" Smith, the bunco artist, was brought up from Denver to conduct his games of chance at the bull ring. Five rows of gambling concessions and bunco games were set up around the race track. In fact, Soapy fleeced so many people of their ticket money that there were many empty seats in the stands.

A special Midland Terminal train brought spectators from Colorado Springs to the depot at Gillett. Joe Wolfe got carried away, and donned a sombrero and serapé to become Señor José Wolfe, the only Jewish matador in Gillett that day. As there was no trumpeter (where was Joe Moore?), a flutist from the Butte Opera House played to call out the first bull. Señor Marrero dispatched one thoroughly confused bull before Sheriff Bowers and the El Paso County SPCA arrived with an arrest warrant.

Wolfe and Meadows were jailed for cruelty to animals. To protect them from angry spectators, Gillett's justice of the peace fined them $5 each and dismissed the charges. Two more bulls were killed on Sunday, the second day. A later trial assessed larger fines, which were paid by Meadows, whose Wild West Show was playing at the Cheyenne Mountain Country Club in Colorado Springs at the time.

Joe Wolfe sold his hotel and left Cripple Creek soon after having put on the only genuine Mexican bull fight ever staged in the United States. There are undocumented rumors that a bull fight occurred once in Dodge City, Kansas, but there is no doubt about the one at Gillett. After a sojurn in Oklahoma, Wolfe went to New York, where he opened a restaurant on Broadway.

So, life among the Cripple Creek miners was varied, sometimes bawdy, but never dull. Life in the mining district continued to flourish well into the 20th century and goes on today. By 1900, gold production had dropped to about $12 million a year. The original 35,000 people had dwindled down to 5,000. Today's population in the last census found 655 persons living in Cripple Creek and another 265 in Victor.

WESTERN HISTORY DEPARTMENT – DENVER PUBLIC LIBRARY

SCENIC, TWISTING PHANTOM CANYON was the route of the narrow-gauge Florence & Cripple Creek Railroad. This line hauled coal, freight and passengers up to the gold camps of the Cripple Creek Mining District. This view was taken by L. C. McClure.

The Iron Horse Comes To Cripple Creek

LTHOUGH CRIPPLE CREEK was not far from Colorado Springs as the crow flies, the 3,482 feet of difference in elevation made access difficult. Ute Pass was the primary route rain. An alternative was the 30-mile-long shelf road that came up Wilson Creek from Cañon City. A third road climbed up through Phantom Canyon from Florence to the Cripple Creek basin.

Some of his friends at the Denver & Rio Grande depot in Florence urged veteran teamster Dave Wood to move his freight and stagecoach operations from Gunnison and the San Juan towns to the Arkansas River Valley, in order to make a connection from the south between Cañon City and Cripple Creek. Such a connection would also be highly profitable for the railroad, as well. If one could rely on public transportation all the way, more people would purchase tickets to the gold camps.

Dave Wood chose the Phantom Canyon route, an improved road that had been financed by Cañon City businessmen to stimulate trade. It was called the "Florence & Cripple Creek Free Road Company," but it did not finish the grade all the way up to Cripple Creek. Cañon City's ardor had cooled suddenly. It was Dave Wood who completed the final leg from Lawrence to Cripple Creek. Wood operated four six-horse Concord stagecoaches over the road each day. Because the road was steep, he changed the animals each 12 miles. The book, *Overland Stage to California*, credits Dave Wood with the first stagecoach line into Cripple Creek. In her book, *Cripple Creek Days*, author Mabel Barbee Lee described how her family got to the gold camps on one of Dave Wood's coaches.

Concord coaches were made in far-away New Hampshire. They were preferred over all other makes for mountain travel since the coach body rested on thick leather straps that never allowed it to touch the frame. This meant that on steep mountain roads, the wheels might be at a precarious angle, but the coach would swing free, like a pendulum of a clock, and find its own center of gravity. Due to primitive road conditions, the ride was hard, and sleep was next to impossible, but the Concords rarely turned over. Mail and packages were secured in a leather "boot" at the rear of the coach.

Stagecoach interiors became rolling saunas when the summer sun beat down. It got worse when the leather curtains were lowered to keep out the ever-present dust. If it rained, passengers got drenched. Food was poor at the swing stations, and toilet facilities did not exist. One lady complained, "Why, there's not even a bush to get behind." Care of passengers on a stage line was secondary to the care of animals.

Probably the greatest single influence in the settlement of Colorado and the West was the coming of the railroads. The difficulties associated with constructing a rail line to a place like Cripple Creek were intimidating. But such a concentration of population, plus the accompanying need for hauling freight, made it desirable, even essential. Building costs were far in excess of the expense of building roads. Railroads were by-products of prosperity. When those persons who controlled capital felt optimistic, the result might mean that a railroad could be built to a Leadville, a Telluride or a Cripple Creek. In the end, the immediate result of railroad building was the real opening-up of Colorado's last frontiers.

Well before the time of the gold discoveries at Cripple Creek, the standard-gauge Colorado Midland Railroad was incorporated, during 1883. Its tracks were extended up Ute Pass from Colorado Springs, across South Park to the Arkansas River Valley. The Midland entered booming Leadville on August 31, 1887. So, some of the people who were headed for Cripple Creek simply rode the Midland Route for $1.50 to Divide. From that point, they rode the Hundley stagecoaches the rest of the way.

To the south, a similar situation prevailed with General Palmer's narrow-gauge Denver & Rio Grande. It had been built south from Denver through Colorado Springs to Pueblo, then west to Florence by the end of 1872. From there, Dave Wood's Concord stagecoaches traversed the 40-mile-long road through Phantom Canyon to Victor.

WESTERN HISTORY DEPARTMENT - DENVER PUBLIC LIBRARY

L. C. McCLURE OF DENVER exposed many glass negatives of the legendary Florence & Cripple Creek Railroad through the scenic Phantom Canyon.

Originally, this grade had been called Eight Mile Canyon, a strange name for a 40-mile-long road. The Phantom Canyon name superseded it at a later time. Suddenly, the Cañon City and Florence business communities began to show an interest in Phantom Canyon once more. Now they were as excited about the railroad as they had formerly been with the earlier stagecoach and freighting road. A railroad would be even better for business. At the peak of the gold excitement, one estimate has suggested that 250 people entered the Cripple Creek country by way of Phantom Canyon each day.

Of the three rail lines that were built into Cripple Creek, the narrow-gauge Florence & Cripple Creek was the first to arrive. It called itself the "Gold Belt Line." On July 1, 1894, its first train steamed up through Phantom Canyon and into Victor. Passengers on that first run had taken the Denver & Rio Grande as far as Florence, where they were able to transfer to the F&CC for the final leg of their journey. From Victor, the track continued through Anaconda and Elkton to the Florence & Cripple Creek depot at the south edge of the city. There had been bets placed as to whether the F&CC or the Midland Terminal would come in first. It was a close race. The Florence & Cripple Creek had won, by just three days.

A parade up Bennett Avenue celebrated the first train's arrival. Both the Anaconda Drum Corp and the Elks Club Band played as people danced on the sidewalks. Presents were handed out from a baggage car, which also brought fresh vegetables, fruit and watermelons from Rocky Ford. After dark, there was a fireworks display. On the return trip to Florence, there was a wreck. The train derailed on the curved trestle above Anaconda and fell 40 feet down the bank. One man was killed, and several were injured.

The Florence & Cripple Creek was the brain child of millionaire David Moffat, who built it at the urging of Winfield Scott Stratton. It was Moffat who drove a golden spike into the last tie. Dave Moffat's fortune came from wise investments in Aspen and Leadville, among other enterprises. It had cost him $800,000 to construct

FROM THE COLLECTION OF EVELYN AND ROBERT L. BROWN

DURING THE 1890'S, Florence, Colorado, was not a very large settlement. A narrow-gauge Florence & Cripple Creek train is shown above, beside the depot (at left), probably loading for a run up to Cripple Creek.

ON THE PHANTOM CANYON LOOP, two trains of the Florence & Cripple Creek are visible. Two little narrow-gauge locomotives — one in front and one at the rear — can be seen on the high grade at the top of the picture below.

WESTERN HISTORY DEPARTMENT - DENVER PUBLIC LIBRARY

FROM THE COLLECTION OF EVELYN AND ROBERT L. BROWN

ON THE RETURN TRIP from Cripple Creek, the first train of the Florence & Cripple Creek went off the wooden trestle at Barry (or Anaconda). Notice the building with the small tower at the right.

THIS COLOR VIEW — taken during 1990 — shows the site of the Florence & Cripple Creek's Anaconda trestle. Notice that the structure with the tower still stands.

FROM THE COLLECTION OF EVELYN AND ROBERT L. BROWN

WESTERN HISTORY DEPARTMENT – DENVER PUBLIC LIBRARY

IN THE VIEW ABOVE, both the words "wreck" and "Rio Grande" are misspelled. Actually, the scene is not on the Rio Grande; it was taken on the Florence & Cripple Creek. And it shows the curious crowd that gathered to view the derailment of the first F&CC at the Anaconda trestle.

AFTER NEGOTIATING Phantom Canyon, the Florence & Cripple Creek's first passenger train was pictured at Victor by James A. Harlan. Strangely, the photographer subsequently spelled his own name incorrectly on his glass negative.

WESTERN HISTORY DEPARTMENT – DENVER PUBLIC LIBRARY

WESTERN HISTORY DEPARTMENT – DENVER PUBLIC LIBRARY

VETERAN DENVER LENSMAN L. C. McClure exposed this well-composed picture of a Florence & Cripple Creek train at the loop in Phantom Canyon. The train was southbound, on a return run from Victor.

AN UNKNOWN PHOTOGRAPHER took this view of two trains on the Florence & Cripple Creek's loop in Phantom Canyon — several miles south of the Cripple Creek Mining District.

WESTERN HISTORY DEPARTMENT – DENVER PUBLIC LIBRARY

WESTERN HISTORY DEPARTMENT – DENVER PUBLIC LIBRARY

L. C. McCLURE OF DENVER exposed many glass negatives of the legendary Florence & Cripple Creek Railroad through the scenic Phantom Canyon.

the Florence & Cripple Creek. Incidentally, it was finished three days ahead of schedule. The final six miles of the steep four-percent grade approaching Victor was accomplished over a series of loops.

Moffat's engineers had the foresight to locate the line along the west side of the mining district, adjacent to the richest mines. Spur tracks were laid to several of the other rich properties. The F&CC proved to be a profitable investment, but just how profitable is open to question. One source insists that construction costs were recovered within the first year of operation. Another source tells us that the costs were not recovered until the end of 18 months. Either way, it was an attractive proposition.

In the beginning, Dave Moffat used leased Rio Grande rolling stock. Three of his trains ran each way every day. Additionally, many passenger runs were made each day on the short six miles of track between Cripple Creek and Victor.

Recently, the origin of the Phantom Canyon name has caused somewhat of a local stir. The popular "Memories" column written by Frances Melrose in the Sunday *Rocky Mountain News* started it. The inquiry prompted a number of responses from her many readers. Supposedly, people have seen ghostly apparitions from time to time, above the canyon's eastern ridge, near Cemetery Park. Another reader told how a man (un-named) followed a ghost horse and dog to the edge of the canyon one night. Later, in daylight, he returned and dug around the spot where the animals had entered the canyon and unearthed the skeletons of a dog and a horse.

A third account involves the Chinese laborers who laid the F&CC's ties and rails during the 1893–1894 construction years. When two loads of dynamite were set off above the second tunnel, a work crew of 30 Chinese men was sent out the following day to clear away the debris. However, the second charge had failed to detonate. Without warning, it exploded while the Chinese track gang was working and buried them on the spot. Other workers steadfastly refused to uncover this last resting place. Later, mournful cries were heard, assumed to have been the spirits of the Celestials in search of peace and rest.

Finally, there is the tale of a Ute maiden who lost her lover in the canyon after they had eloped. On nights that are still, it is said that she can be heard, even now, mourning for her lost love. Why have spiritualist mediums never discovered Phantom Canyon?

Although the Florence & Cripple Creek was a very profitable railroad, its life span was brief, a mere 18 years. Because of its steep grades, this had always been a rather costly line to operate. On July 30, 1912, a sudden flash flood roared down through Phantom Canyon, destroying 18 bridges and almost 10 miles of track. Earlier, in 1899, the astute Moffat had sold the Florence & Cripple Creek to the rival Midland Terminal line. That very next year, Colorado Springs replaced Florence as the primary refining center for Cripple Creek's ores. For the railroad, that 1912 flood had merely put on the finishing touches. By 1918, the Phantom Canyon route had become a scenic but dusty automobile road. Even now, most of it remains unpaved.

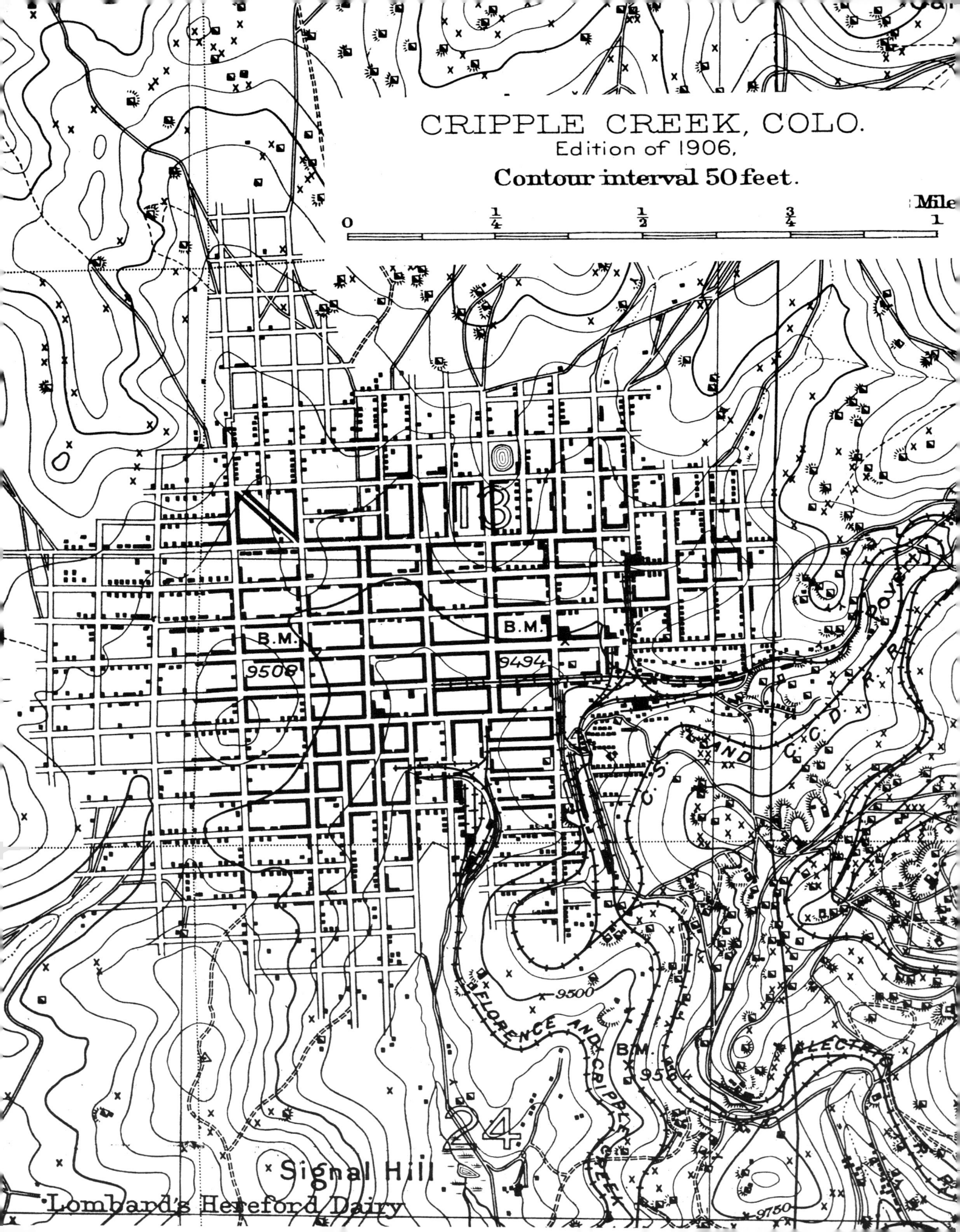

FROM THE COLLECTION OF FREDA AND FRANCIS B. RIZZARI

IN CRIPPLE CREEK we see a Florence & Cripple Creek train crossing the wye across Poverty Gulch. The Midland Terminal's depot shows left of center.

ALTHOUGH THE TRESTLES across Poverty Gulch have now been filled with mine tailings, its original contours, as well as the depot at Cripple Creek, can still be seen.

FROM THE COLLECTION OF EVELYN AND ROBERT L. BROWN

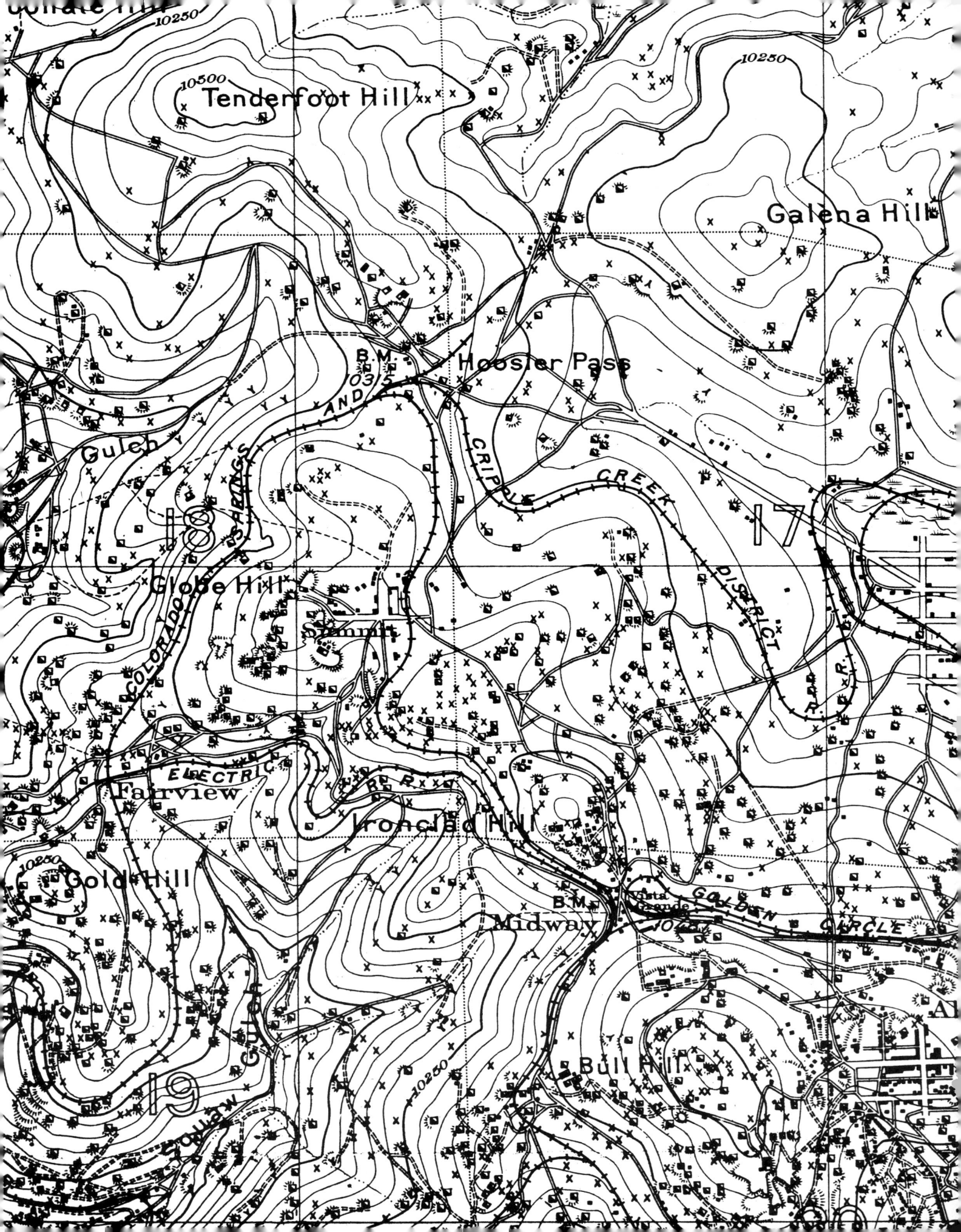

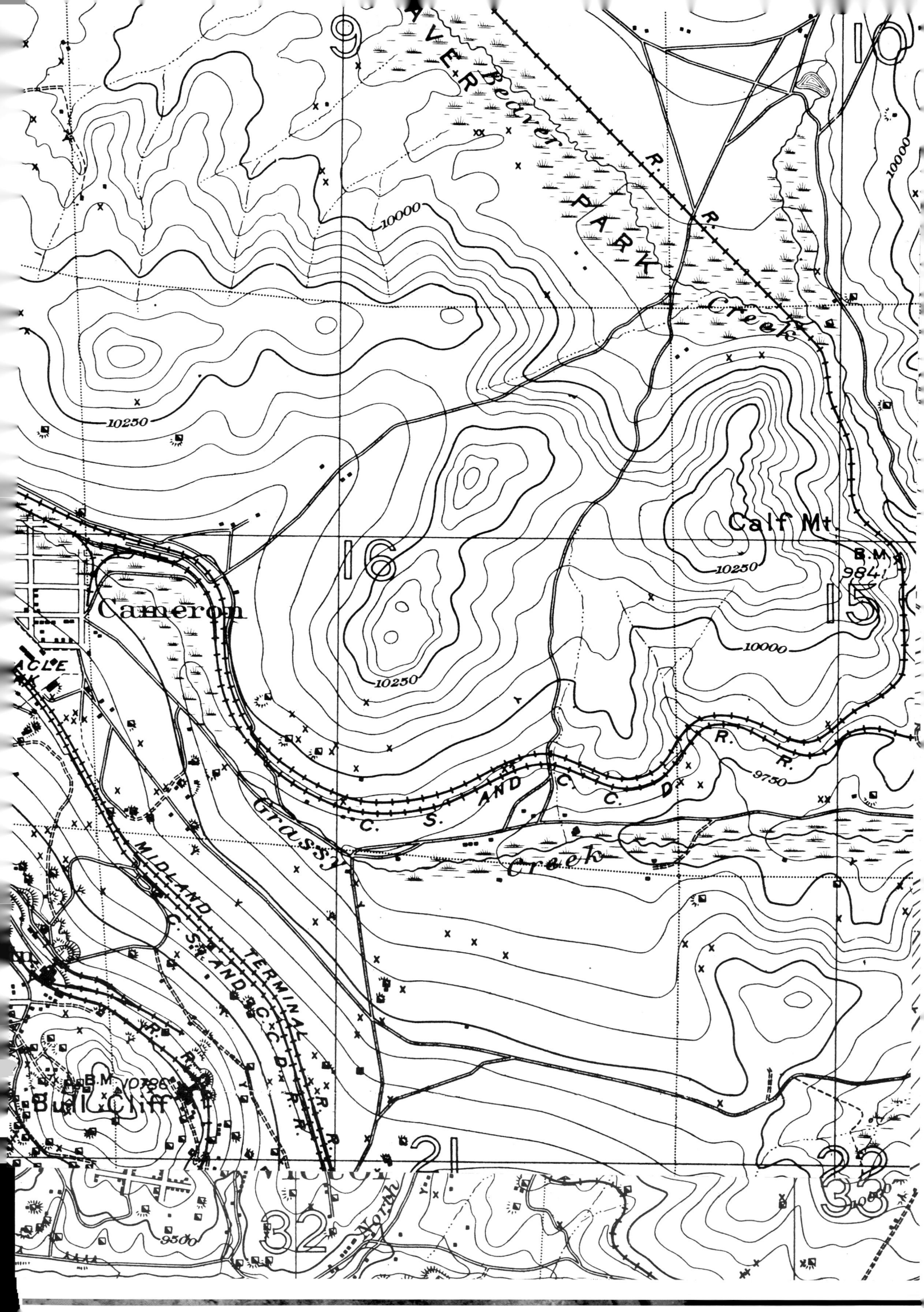

FROM THE COLLECTION OF EVELYN AND ROBERT L. BROWN

IF YOU DRIVE OVER the Gold Camp Road for 8.6 miles, you will arrive at Saint Peters Dome. Today, the Pike National Forest maintains a short hiking path to the top of the dome.

REPRODUCED BELOW is a contemporary color picture of Saint Peters Dome. Notice that the same two large rocks at the left are still in place.

FROM THE COLLECTION OF EVELYN AND ROBERT L. BROWN

CATHEDRAL ROCKS—THE CRIPPLE CREEK TRIP

FROM THE COLLECTION OF EVELYN AND ROBERT L. BROWN

THE PINK SANDSTONE formations in Cathedral Park constituted one of the most inspiring sights on the Short Line. On weekends, this was a favorite picnic spot, a short 22.6 miles up from Colorado Springs.

TODAY, THE CATHEDRAL ROCKS have not changed. In the autumn, this spot is a prime location for aspen "leaf peepers" (sightseers). The entire route to Cripple Creek is colorful during the fall.

FROM THE COLLECTION OF EVELYN AND ROBERT L. BROWN

but finally, the competing lines called a halt to the rate war. Incidentally, the CS&CCD also owned the district's two electric interurban trolley-car routes, the High Line and the Low Line.

Profits in the years after the turn of the century were not that great, and in 1905, the Short Line's owners decided to avoid bankruptcy by selling the whole operation to the Colorado & Southern Railway (now part of the vast Burlington Northern). Almost at once, the C&S leased it to the Midland Terminal. All service ended for both the railroad and the two interurban lines in 1920.

W. D. Corley purchased the abandoned right-of-way in 1924, junked the rails and ties, and turned the grade into a toll road, to be known as the Corley Mountain Highway. When Corley's franchise ran out, the road reverted to the public domain, and it has been know as the Gold Camp Road since that time.

Today, this road ranks as one of the finest drives on a preserved and maintained railroad grade in all of North America. The original grade has been followed faithfully, except for a few slight deviations in the interest of safety. In its heyday, Cripple Creek's gold provided an extended period of lucrative profits for the owners of these three unusual mountain railroads.

FROM THE COLLECTION OF EVELYN AND ROBERT L. BROWN

AT THE HEIGHT of the gold boom and before the two fires, Cripple Creek's population reached about 35,000, with some 50,000 in the entire mining district. Bennett and Myers avenues — the two principal streets in Cripple Creek — run diagonally across the picture, which was taken from Globe Hill.

The District's Fires

HE LATE AUTHOR, Muriel Sibell Wolle, once told me that at least one major fire swept most mining towns. Fairplay and Breckenridge escaped, as did Georgetown, which had an unusually good fire department. Cripple Creek burned twice within the brief time span of one week. It was just a routine Saturday morning, on April 25, 1896, when one of Spencer Penrose's favorite bartenders from the Topic Saloon finished his night shift, and was making his way up to a room that he shared with one of "the girls." The room was on the second floor, above the Central Dance Hall, at Third and Myers Avenue.

There is a discount on just how the conflagration began. One story asserts that there was a disagreement over the price, and she threw a lighted oil lamp at him. The barman ducked, and the lamp broke beside a window, setting fire to the curtains. A second version seems more plausible. There was an argument, and it became physical when the man slapped the girl's face. She retaliated by attacking him with a large knife. In the inevitable donnybrook that followed, a gasoline stove was upset onto the dry plank floor. A few minutes later, the entire frame structure was aflame. It burned quickly. Both of the pugilists fled the scene. Neither their names nor the nature of their dispute has survived.

At the time of the fire, most of Cripple Creek was composed of the old original wooden frame buildings, and they were tinder dry. To make matters worse, a brisk wind was blowing, quickly spreading the fire to the two-story Topic Saloon next door. Three parlor houses and six cribs were consumed as the wind continued to spread the flames. Most of the structures along Myers Avenue went up in smoke. Several frail sisters exited second and third story rooms by ropes, which had been tossed up by town firemen. Puppies, kittens and other pets, along with cherished stashes of laudanum, were dropped to friends on the sidewalk below.

Lacking a conventional fire alarm, the dreaded six pistol shots in succession were heard, spreading the warning across the community. Cripple Creek's single pumper was pulled to the hot spots by two big Percheron horses. For nearly three-quarters of an hour, fire fighters were able to keep the destruction contained to Myers Avenue, but the effort exhausted water reserves in the reservoir, and hose pressure dropped. Firemen protected themselves from the toxic smoke by breathing through moistened sponges.

Victor sent its fire department, but it arrived too late to save Cripple Creek. By this time, the smoke plume was so massive that it was visible down in Colorado Springs. Firemen used dynamite on a 200-foot-wide swath of fragile structures that stood in the fire's path, creating fire breaks, which they hoped would halt the spread of the fiery destruction.

However, the fire break failed to work, as the flames jumped across Dance Hall Alley to begin licking at the backs of structures on the south side of Bennett Avenue. Two banks, several businesses, the post office and a number of the higher class saloons on Bennett Avenue were destroyed. Now, the fire turned north, burning four churches and a number of the fine homes on Carr and Eaton avenues. When the wind abated, the fire was contained, but eight blocks between Third and Fifth streets were gone. In all, it had lasted for three hours.

Although some 5,000 persons were without shelter, recovery began almost at once. Many businesses and a gospel tent re-opened under canvas that night, including several brothels, which opened up inside hastily erected single-room cribs. There is one account of a "cat wagon" that arrived two days after the fire. It was a hastily improvised vehicle, modeled after the rolling brothels that moved from town to town during the cowboy period in Kansas. "Cat wagons" were large vehicles, which contained six curtained bunks on either side of a narrow center aisle.

Cripple Creek's newspaper cleaned up its press and moved to another location to produce the Sunday edition right on schedule. Down in Colorado Springs, Winfield Scott Stratton formed a hasty relief committee and sent two trainloads of food and building supplies on special

FROM THE COLLECTION OF EVELYN AND ROBERT L. BROWN

DURING THE VICTOR FIRE the Florence & Cripple Creek Railroad urged people to load their personal belongings into a series of empty cars. When full, the train backed into the rock cut beyond the reach of the fire. This is an E. A. Yelton photograph.

Midland Terminal trains. Father Volpe opened Saint Peter's Catholic Church as a shelter for mothers and small children. In all, 30 acres of the town had been destroyed.

The following Wednesday, it happened all over again. At Second Street and Myers Avenue, one of the cooks in the old Portland Hotel upset a kettle of grease onto a hot stove, and flames quickly shot up the stovepipe. Once again, there was a wind, and the fire spread until it had engulfed the entire structure. Sparks from the Portland spread to the Palace, where a boiler exploded, and to a grocery store, where some 700 pounds of dynamite detonated with a thunderous roar. Ten saloons were burned to the ground, along with a bank, a harness shop, a restaurant, a laundry and a livery stable. That night, looters appeared and carried off anything of value that they could find. Some of them were apprehended by the police.

Once again, Stratton put together a rescue committee and sent relief supplies up on a special train. Money poured in from New York, San Francisco, Denver, and from as far away as London. The second fire pretty well finished off what the first one had started. But it may have been a blessing in disguise, as the original structures were dry, had never been painted and were a fire hazard. In a very real sense, the fire ended the era of shacks in Cripple Creek. In order to preclude a recurrence, most of the replacement structures along Bennett Avenue were of stone and brick construction. Only the cribs up in Poverty Gulch and some cabins at the south end of the city had been missed by the fire.

Victor burned, too, in August of 1899. As at Cripple Creek, the fire started in a dancehall, which was called the "999," owned by Jennie Thompson. It seems that one of Jennie's soiled doves was cleaning a dress with gasoline while smoking! Most of the commercial district between First and Fifth streets, and between Granite and Portland avenues, went up in flames. Fourteen blocks

FROM THE COLLECTION OF EVELYN AND ROBERT L. BROWN

FROM THE SAME ANGLE as the Yelton picture, the highway from Cripple Creek now passes through this rock cut. Above the cut, several of the same homes can be seen.

FROM THE COLLECTION OF EVELYN AND ROBERT L. BROWN

FROM THE IDENTICAL ANGLE as the Harlan fire picture, this recent color shot shows the same houses at the lower left. Note how the burned section was rebuilt, with brick structures.

Remains of Victor Colo Next Day after the Fire
A.J. Harlan Photo. Aug 22, 99.

FROM THE COLLECTION OF EVELYN AND ROBERT L. BROWN

THIS HARLAN PICTURE was taken the morning after the Victor fire. The homes at the lower left were untouched by the inferno.

were destroyed in about two hours. Two railroad depots burned, as did the surface structures of the Gold Coin mine. Another of the buildings that was lost was the Gold Coin Club, where Jack Dempsey boxed a couple of times.

As you enter Victor today, the burned-out area is still clearly visible, as all of the buildings that have taken place of those that were destroyed are of brick and stone. The damage amounted to about $1 million. Some 3,000 people were left homeless by the fire.

Over in Squaw Gulch, the town of Anaconda was fourth in size among the district's towns. Anaconda's fire destroyed the town in its entirety. It happened in the winter of 1904. Reservoirs were frozen, and the town's wells were useless. So hot was the blaze that even the wooden power poles were aflame. Curiously, nobody seemed interested in rebuilding Anaconda. Its residents apparently salvaged what they could, and then moved to Goldfield, Victor or Cripple Creek.

At present, Squaw Gulch is a barren scar, bisected by a single road. One fire hydrant still keep its forlorn vigil, and a stone corner of the jail can still be seen. North of the townsite is the tailings dump of the big Anaconda mine. On the hillside, above the scar that was Anaconda's main street, stands the huge cribbed-up tailings pile of the Mary McKinney mine and some other properties that were untouched by the fire. Otherwise, Anaconda is little more than a memory.

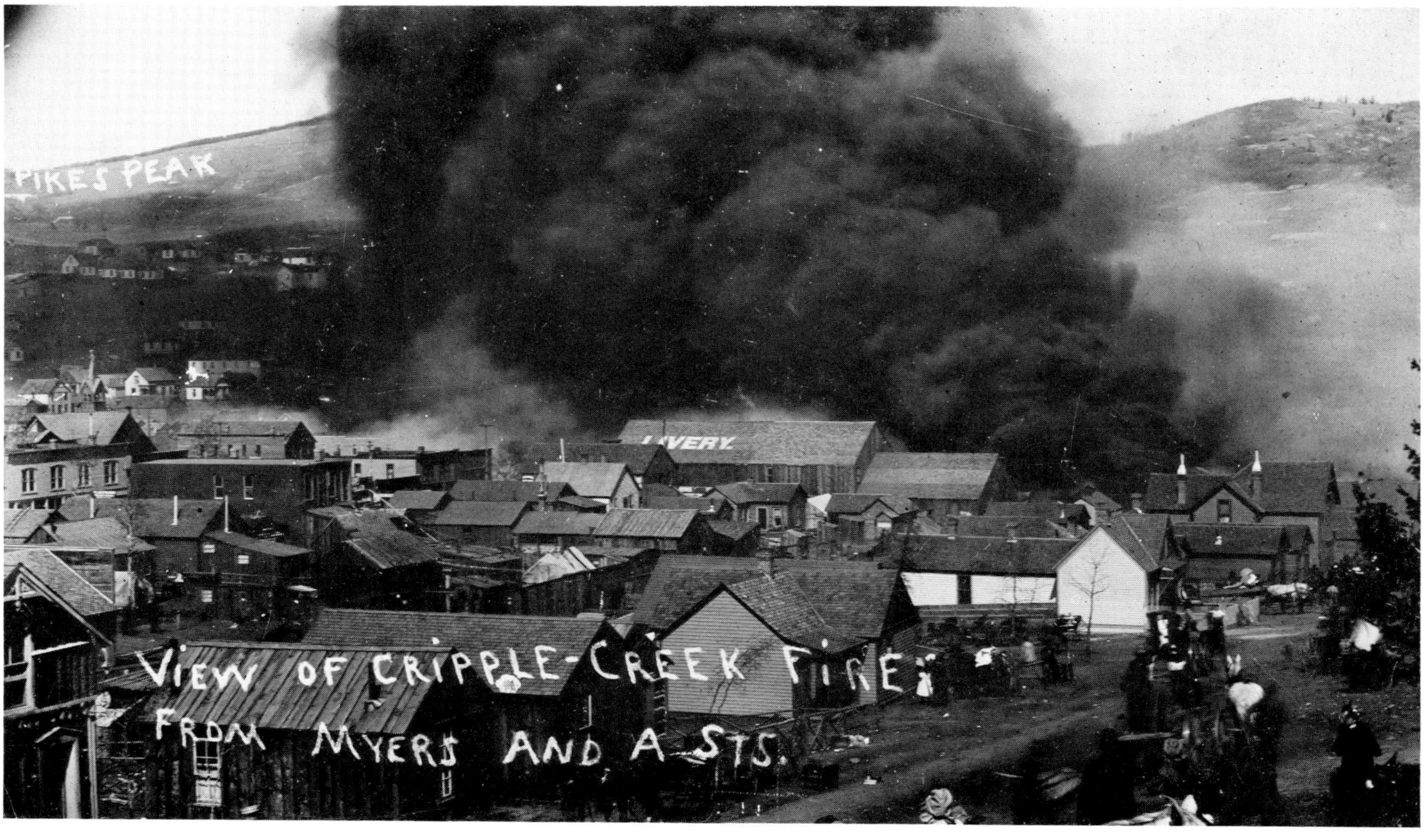
PIKES PEAK
LIVERY
VIEW OF CRIPPLE-CREEK FIRE
FROM MYERS AND A STS.

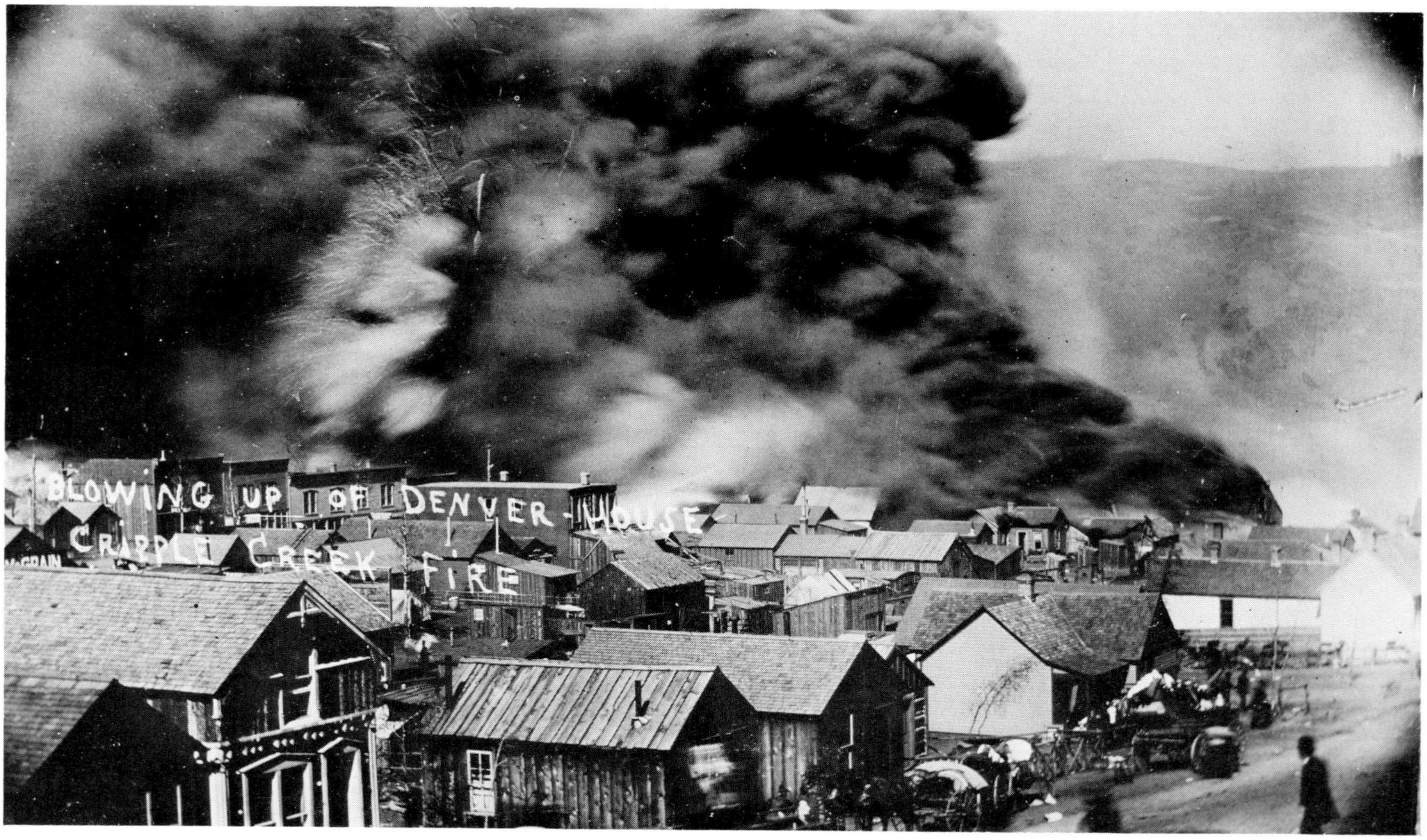
BLOWING UP OF DENVER-HOUSE
CRIPPLE CREEK FIRE

FROM THE COLLECTION OF EVELYN AND ROBERT L. BROWN

IN THIS THIRD PICTURE the hole in the roof of the livery stable is seen. Foreground structures in all three pictures are some of the Myers Avenue "cribs."

FROM THE COLLECTION OF EVELYN AND ROBERT L. BROWN

E. A. YELTON EXPOSED a series of three plates from the junction of Myers Avenue and "A" Street. Unknown to anyone, a quantity of dynamite was stored in the livery stable.

FROM THE COLLECTION OF EVELYN AND ROBERT L. BROWN

ALTHOUGH YELTON'S CAPTION labels this scene as the "blowing up of the Denver House," actually it was the dynamite that exploded in the stable.

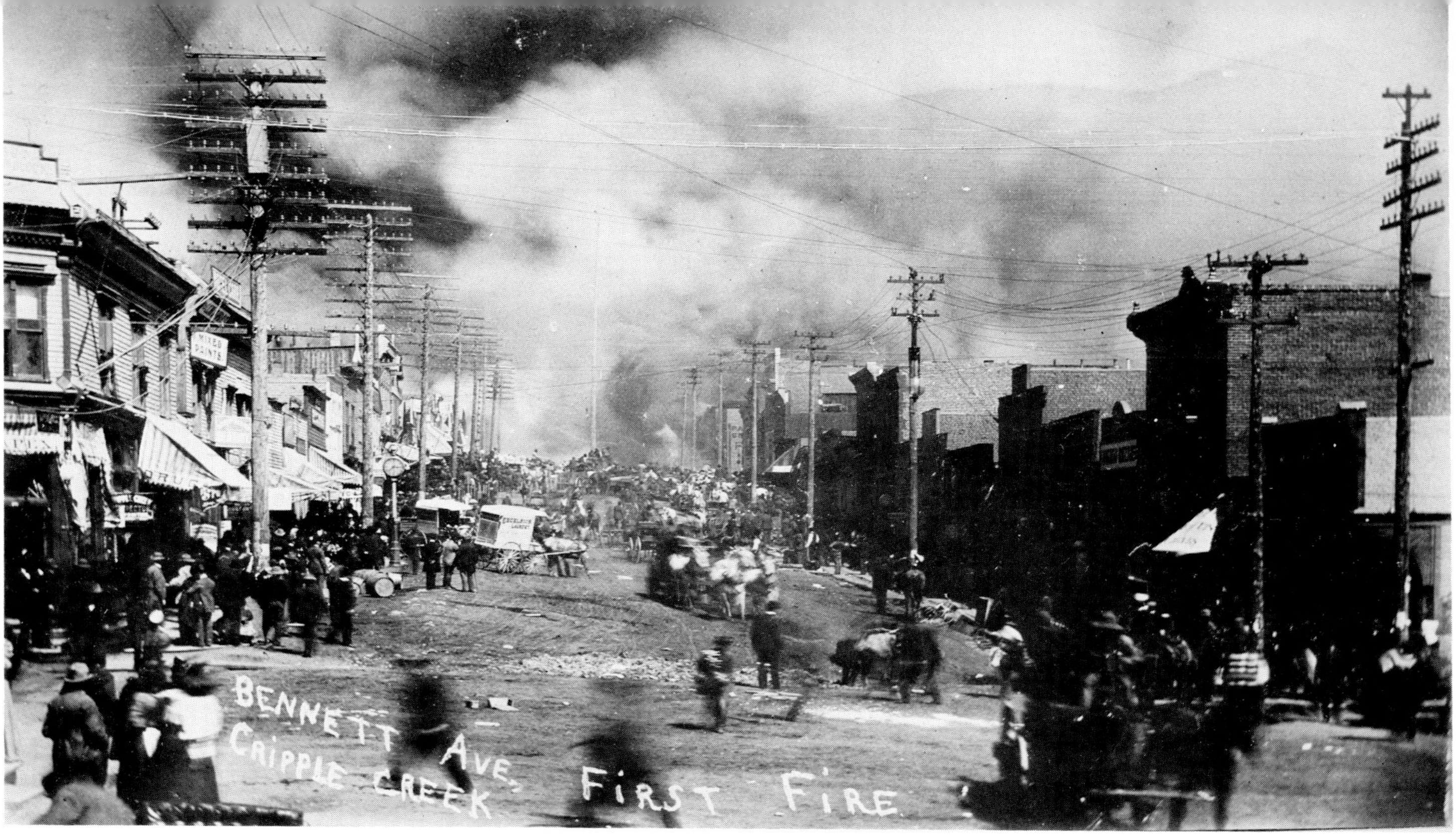

FROM THE COLLECTION OF EVELYN AND ROBERT L. BROWN

WHEN CRIPPLE CREEK'S big fire began on Myers Avenue, the flames spread quickly over the city. This view looks east at the total confusion on Bennett Avenue.

HOSE-CART RACES between rival fire companies were a popular form of recreation. Bennett Avenue is the scene of this contest.

FROM THE COLLECTION OF EVELYN AND ROBERT L. BROWN

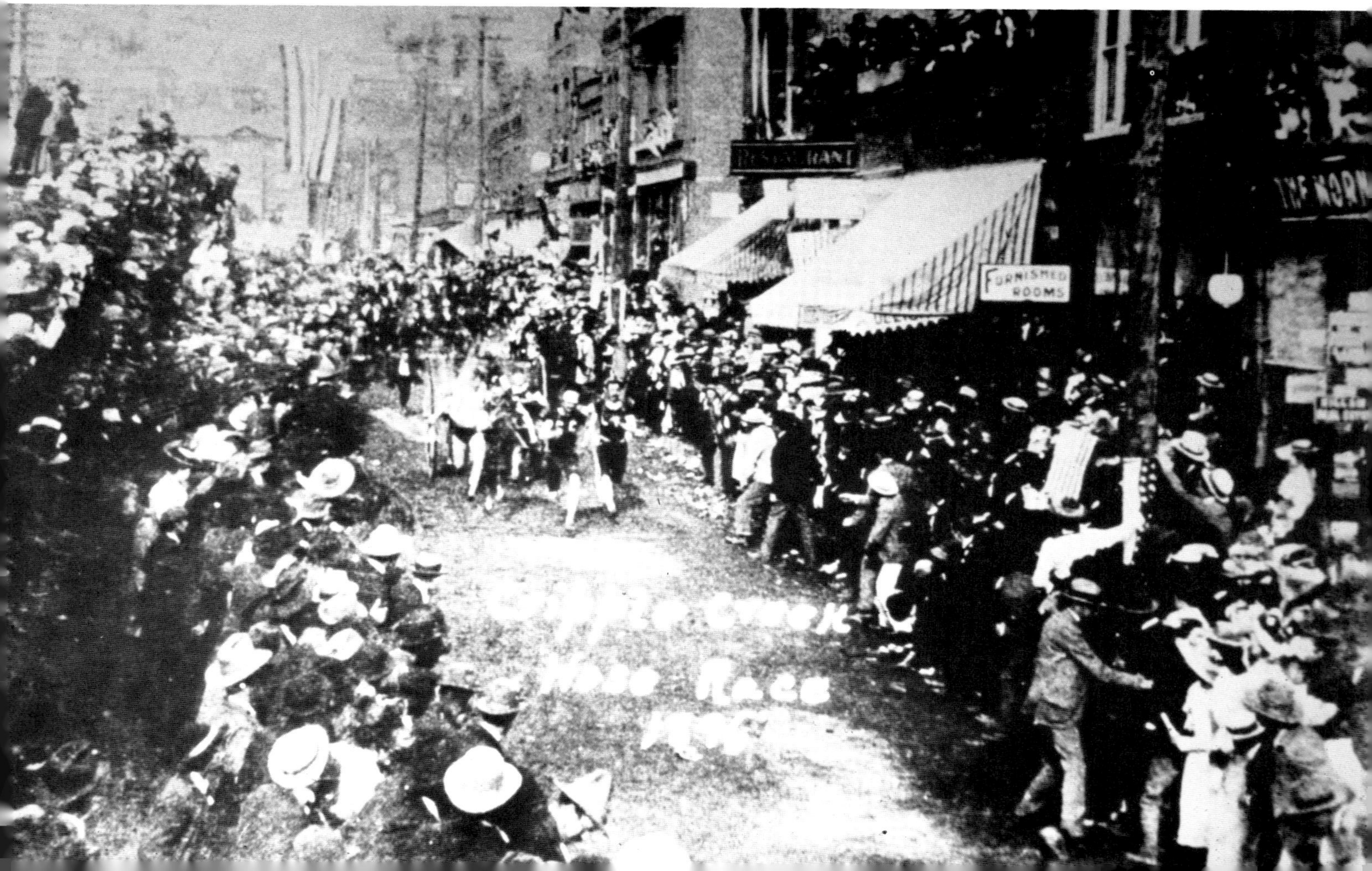

FROM THE COLLECTION OF EVELYN AND ROBERT L. BROWN

HERE IS ANOTHER E. A. Yelton picture of the Victor fire. Notice the enormous smoke pall, the furniture in the foreground and the man carrying his mattress. Many people kept their money in their mattresses at this time.

THIS MODERN PICTURE matches the Yelton fire photograph. Notice that many of the same houses at the left survived the blaze.

FROM THE COLLECTION OF EVELYN AND ROBERT L. BROWN

LIBRARY – COLORADO HISTORICAL SOCIETY

GOLDFIELD WAS A STRONG union town. Here, the Colorado militia practices a saber drill, a favorite fetish of the military.

FROM THE COLLECTION OF EVELYN AND ROBERT L. BROWN

BULKLEY WELLS was a captain in the Colorado National Guard who saw duty in Cripple Creek during the labor wars.

Labor Wars at the Turn of the Century

IN COMMON with fires, one of the less pleasant happenings that occurred in the history of a number of Colorado's mining districts was the tragic struggle between workers and mine owners. The dominant issues that usually brought matters to an impasse were pay scales, living and working conditions, and the length of the work day. At Cripple Creek, there were two strikes, in 1894, and again in 1903. Taken together, they are sometimes referred to as the "Turn of the Century Labor Wars."

Following the economic effects of the nation-wide Panic of 1893, a four-year period of hard times swept the country. It was a particularly rough time here in the West. Silver-mining areas closed down from Leadville through Aspen to the San Juan region. Since gold was now the pre-eminent metal, out-of-work miners from the silver-mining towns flocked to Cripple Creek, creating a labor surplus that could benefit only the mine owners.

Once again, the classic cleavage between the "haves" and the "have nots" took center stage. Most mine owners were Colorado Springs Episcopalians and Republicans, while at least one-third of the workers were Irish Catholics. A majority of the frustrations of the of the miners surfaced at Altman, where lumberman Sam Altman had platted a town astride the 10,620-foot-high summit between Bull Hill and Bull Cliff. The going rate of pay was $3 for nine hours of work.

For a better understanding of the events to follow, a few observations about the leading personalities may be helpful at this point. To begin with, there was Governor Davis H. Waite, a 67-year-old Aspen attorney and justice of the peace. Waite was a former Democrat who became a Republican shortly after his arrival in Colorado in 1879. He had a wild, flowing white mane and beard that made him look like an Old Testament prophet who had survived a strike by lightning. In Aspen, he founded a newspaper, *The Aspen Union Era*, and changed his politics for the third time. He joined the Populist Party. Waite favored an income tax, the eight-hour work day, the secret ballot, and the direct, popular election of U.S. senators.

During 1892, Waite became the only Populist in America to be elected as a governor. Later that same year, he achieved a degree of notoriety by exclaiming in public, "It is infinitely better that blood should flow to our horses' bridles than our national liberties should be destroyed." After unleashing that gem, he was known across the state as "Old Bloody Bridles Waite."

When government silver purchases ended in 1893, Governor Waite proposed that Colorado should buy up surplus silver at the old price to be sent to Mexico, where cheap labor would mint it into "Fandango Dollars," to be circulated in the state. Waite was blamed for a variety of things, including the strikes at Cripple Creek, and was not re-elected.

William Dudley Haywood was a Socialist. Physically, he was a huge man, and people called him "Big Bill." Walter Wellman of Chicago's *Record Herald* called him "one of the smartest men I ever knew." Many writers attribute the violence that the public has come to associate with the labor movement to "Big Bill" Haywood. He held the office of secretary in the Western Federation of Miners, but his influence extended far beyond his modest title. "Big Bill" referred to Colorado's Adjutant General Sherman Bell as "an insane man in gold lace." His term for the National Guard was "tin soldiers." It was Haywood who recruited and trained Harry Orchard, one of the most violent men in all of America's turbulent labor history.

Albert E. Horsley was a cheese maker from Ontario, Canada, who had migrated south to Idaho's Coeur d'Alene mining district. There, he changed his name to Harry Orchard, in order to escape an unhappy marriage. "Big Bill" recognized a degree of ruthlessness in Orchard that fitted into the union's plans. Governor Frank Steunenberg of Idaho had called out the state militia to break a strike at Coeur d'Alene, where Orchard had blown up the Gem mine. So, Haywood let a contract to Orchard, who killed the governor with a dynamite blast at Steunenberg's home on December 30, 1905. Harry Orchard's string of murders for the union totaled about 20. In 1904, Haywood ordered Harry into Cripple Creek. He lived at Independence, and collected money each week to help pay the preacher's salary.

James H. Peabody, a Cañon City businessman, was

COLLECTION OF FREDA AND FRANCIS B. RIZZARI

ALTMAN WAS NOT only the highest town in the district, but it was also headquarters for the Western Federation of Miners. Tents of the Colorado militia are at the lower right.

WHEN THE VICTOR RECORD pleaded for an end to the strike, a contingent of the mine-owner's militia marched the editor and his assistant up the street at gunpoint. Note the crowd across the street who "do not want to get involved".

FROM THE COLLECTION OF EVELYN AND ROBERT L. BROWN

FROM THE COLLECTION OF EVELYN AND ROBERT L. BROWN

AT VICTOR, here is the Vindicator mine. Union-paid assasin Harry Orchard dynamited the Vindicator to discourage non-union workers.

Colorado's governor between 1903 and 1905. The ultra-conservative Peabody was a Republican. In common with Davis Waite in the earlier strike, Governor Peabody also sent the state militia up to Cripple Creek during 1903–1904, but for a totally different reason. Waite had been strongly pro-labor, while Peabody sided with the mine owners, as well as with the financiers who backed the owners. Governor Peabody said that "...the Western Federation of Miners produced more trouble and expense than all other causes combined, including the Indian Wars." He also stated, "We made war on the WFM because it first made war on society!"

And then, there was Scottish-born John Calderwood, one of the unhappiest of the Altman miners. He was also an organizer for the Western Federation of Miners. Soon, Calderwood had recruited all of the Bull Hill men into his Free Coinage Union, No. 19. In the vernacular of the owners, Calderwood's crew was known as the "Bull Hill dynamiters." Holding out a promise of $3 for only eight hours of work enabled him to sign up an additional 800 men from some of the other towns. When the owners resisted, Calderwood called a strike for February of 1894. The owners retaliated by increasing the work day to 10 hours, with no increase in pay.

Only Stratton and Jimmy Burns respected Calderwood and signed with the union. Unemployed silver miners were hired to replace some 3,500 strikers from about 50 mines. Armed guards were retained to protect both the mines and the new workers.

An unusual amount of bitterness, dirty tricks and acts of terrorism accompanied both strikes. Union men shot up Myers Avenue saloons and parlor houses for no particular reason, and they attacked the homes of non-union workers. When two

FROM THE COLLECTION OF FRED AND JO MAZZULLA

SHOWN HERE is union assasin Harry Orchard. Orchard lived at the town of Independence during the strike.

FROM THE COLLECTION OF EVELYN AND ROBERT L. BROWN

THE TROOPERS stationed here called their cantonment "Camp Goldfield." The town is seen on the hillside.

THIS SO-CALLED "PEABODY MEDAL" was issued to troopers who broke strikes at the places listed at the top, above the ribbon. Both the back and front of the medal are shown in these views.

FROM THE COLLECTION OF EVELYN AND ROBERT L. BROWN

alleged spies for the mine's proprietors were caught at Altman, they were taken to a saloon and forced to drink deeply from cuspidors. Having survived that indignity, the spies were threatened with having useful parts of their anatomies cut off. Finally, some union men tossed them down an 18 foot deep mine shaft. At one point, mine owners hired a Mrs. Harlie Miller to go to bed with various strikers in order to worm information out of them. But she was frequently too intoxicated to realize with whom she was bedded, so that idea was abandoned.

John Calderwood was an old friend of Governor Waite. So, when El Paso County Sheriff Frank Bowers telephoned the governor for help, the militia, under the inept General Thomas Tarsney, boarded trains, arriving in Cripple Creek on March 18. Getting union men off Bull Hill and out of Altman became a top priority. Sheriff Bowers and his deputies had arrested several unionists, but they were acquitted by Colorado Springs judges. Upon release, they returned to Altman and mined the roads into the "Little Kingdom of Bull Hill."

It was Irving Howbert who remembered that ex-policemen and firemen from Denver hated Waite for firing them during the City Hall War. One-hundred and twenty-five of them were hired and deputized to attack Bull Hill and embarrass Waite. They rode the Colorado Midland and Midland Terminal lines as far as the town of Midland. Under the cover of darkness, they marched the rest of the way into Cripple Creek.

Meanwhile, a log fort had been erected on the crest of Bull Cliff. Fake cannons had been fabricated and pointed toward the town of Victor down below. A crude bow gun propelled beer bottles filled with dynamite down the hill toward the

FROM THE COLLECTION OF ED AND NANCY BATHKE

THE SOMEWHAT OBSCURE TOWN of Midland consisted of little more than a hotel, some homes and was a station on the Midland Terminal line. In the foreground are several heavily armed men. The picture was made during the strike.

JAMES A. HARLAN exposed this glass plate of the town of Altman, besieged by the tented Colorado militia in the foreground.

FROM THE COLLECTION OF EVELYN AND ROBERT L. BROWN

hired mercenaries. Up at Altman, the miners loaded a flatcar with explosives and rolled it downhill toward the Denver force. It jumped the tracks on a curve, exploded and killed two cows. Finally, the Denver deputies capured five strikers. The whole event, worthy of a Gilbert and Sullivan operetta, has been called the "Battle of Bull Hill."

Before it was over, Governor Waite made a personal pilgrimage up to Altman, where he was authorized to arbitrate for the union men. Peace came on June 10, 1894, and the agreement was signed at Altman, ending 130 days of turmoil. So great was the union's hatred toward Adjutant General Tarsney that a ruse was contrived later that same month to get him outside of Colorado Springs' Hotel Alamo. There, he was seized and taken out of town, where tar and feathers were applied. Tarsney was abandoned beside the northbound railroad tracks to walk toward Denver.

The union had won the $3, eight-hour work day, but they lost the next round in the second strike. By that time, "Bloody Bridles" Waite had been turned out of office. The conservative James H. Peabody now occupied the governor's office, and his sympathies were not with the Western Federation of Miners.

Charles Moyers, president of the WFM, called the

second strike in August of 1903. Nine union men, who worked in the non-union Colorado Reduction & Refining Company's mill at Colorado City, were fired for union activity. They had demanded the eight hour day. Moyers and "Big Bill" Haywood reasoned that a strike there by their more than 3,300 miners up at Cripple Creek would cut off the supply of ore to the non-union reduction plant and whip them into line. Once again, the eight hour day had become an issue.

At first, the owners obtained a court order outlawing union interference. As a second step, they ordered a total shut-down at their properties. But with an available and hungry surplus of out-of-work silver miners, their mines were re-opened with I.D. card-carrying non-union help.

But, this time around, there was a new element present in the person of Harry Orchard. While in residence at Independence, Harry worked in, became familiar with, and did some high-grading in several of the larger mines. He called high-grading "...something good for the pockets." Haywood offered $500 if Orchard would blow up the Vindicator mine at Victor. But Harry must have attended a Progressive School, because he mistook the 6th level for the 7th, where work was going on, and he placed his charge there. On November 21, two supervisors went to the 6th level to inspect the stoping. Opening the door pulled the wire that set off Orchard's infernal device, and both men were killed.

But the two events that really brought down Governor Peabody's wrath on the union were the severe beating of a justice of the peace from Anaconda and Harry Orchard's dynamiting of the railroad depot at the station of Independence. On June 5, in company with a miner, named Steve Adams, Harry planted two boxes of explosives under the depot's loading platform. They would be detonated by acid vials when a wire was pulled. At 2:15 A.M. a train carrying the night shift from A. E. Carlton's Findley mine pulled in, and 27 men got off onto the poorly-lighted platform. While hidden in a secluded spot nearby, Harry pulled the wire. Rocks and body parts rained down as the explosion illuminated the night. Thirteen men were killed instantly, and 20 others were badly maimed. The extra six in the body count were railroad employees. One body was found 150 feet away. Some lives were saved by amputations. Six widow were left with 11 children.

Bloodhounds were brought in to track the killers, but Adams and Orchard had soaked their shoes in turpentine and had scattered pepper in their tracks. Adams fled toward Midway, while Orchard made his way to Denver to be paid before going on to Wyoming. The violence continued. Fifteen men were killed when a mine-shaft lift (an elevator) was tampered with in Stratton's Independence mine. On June 7, Governor Peabody responded by declaring martial law. Peabody dispatched the Colorado militia under Adjutant General Sherman Bell to protect life and property in Cripple Creek. The troops were stationed at known locations where trouble might be expected, places such as Goldfield, Altman, where large numbers of union men lived.

One of the prominent members of Colorado's National Guard at this time was the charismatic, handsome, controversial and wealthy Bulkley Wells, who played a significant role in the bloody labor-management violence at Telluride during 1902. He was the son-in-law of the millionaire owner of Telluride's famous Smuggler-Union mining complex. He enlisted in the Colorado militia in 1900, after becoming the manager of his father-in-law's rich mine in Pandora (adjacent to Telluride). Wells was a natural leader, and he loved uniforms. He already held the rank of captain when he rode with his troops into Cripple Creek. By the time he resigned from the militia in 1917, he was a brigadier general. Bulkley Wells left Colorado during 1921, in disgrace over the divorce his wife forced on him due to his adultery. He lived in Utah, Nevada and California for the next decade. After losing all his financial resources, he ended his life in San Francisco on May 26, 1931. He laid down on a couch and shot himself in the head. Wells was only 59 years of age at his death.

Infantry, cavalry and artillery troops were quartered at Goldfield, which also served as headquarters for the militia. General Bell was both the joy and pride of the governor. Bell defied the courts, threatened to jail judges, closed down **The Victor Record** newspaper and arrested editor George Hyner, who had pleaded for understanding and for an end to the strike. The physical plant of the newspaper was vandalized with sledge hammers. Transportation routes, both roads and railroads, were barricaded.

Following Harry Orchard's bombing of the Independence depot, public indignation toward the union reached a fever pitch. Union stores and meeting places were destroyed, and a mass hanging was suggested. Only cool heads kept local vigilantes from stringing up union bodies on power poles in Cripple Creek and Victor.

Instead of lynchings by the "Local Uplift Society," mass arrests of known union members and sympathizers followed. Bull pens, with armed guards, were established to contain them in Victor, Goldfield and Independence. Illegal deportations without trials followed. About 225 men were marched aboard railroad cars. Trains hauled them to the New Mexico and Kansas state borders, where they were marched across at gunpoint. Each man was handed a can of bully beef, 12 hardtacks, a can of beans and a container of water. Seventy-three others were abandoned on eastern Colorado's prairie. Forty-two were held over for trial. Another 200 were imprisoned, while an unknown number fled into the mountains.

By midsummer of 1904, it was all over; the strike had ended. The mines were open once more, with non-union workers, who toiled for nine hours a day for $3. Round-the-clock shifts were standard. As a result of the strike, 33 men were dead. Martial law had been declared, the press was silenced, and freedom of speech and assembly were abolished in the process. The Western Federation of Miners never recovered in Colorado

John Calderwood was tried in Denver and acquitted. Davis Waite died of paralysis in 1901, while peeling apples in the kitchen of his home in Aspen. "Big Bill" Haywood fled to Russia, where he died in exile in 1928. Harry Orchard outlived nearly all of his contemporaries and the WFM, as well. He had assumed the name of Hogan by the time he was arrested in January of 1906, at the Saratoga Hotel in Caldwell, Idaho. Since his first big crime was the Steunenberg murder, he was tried and incarcerated at Point of the Mountains Prison in Idaho. He remained there for nearly half a century, until his death at the age of 88, on April 13, 1954. At this writing, the mansion of Governor James H. Peabody still stands at 1128 Grant Street in Denver. During Halloween it is believed by some to be haunted by the unhappy former governor, who still stalks the halls.

FROM THE COLLECTION OF EVELYN AND ROBERT L. BROWN

THIS "BULL PEN" was cordoned off in Victor to contain union miners prior to deportation from Colorado. Note the spectators, the people who did not get caught, who gathered to observe those who did get caught.

SINCE ELKTON was a hotbed of union activity, a contingent of the Colorado State Militia was stationed there during the strike.

LIBRARY – COLORADO HISTORICAL SOCIETY

99

FROM THE COLLECTION OF EVELYN AND ROBERT L. BROWN

BRILLIANT THEODORE ROOSEVELT, youngest president who ever served the U.S., loved Cripple Creek, and he visited it at least twice. The inset shows a button for the Theodore Roosevelt Club of Denver.

Cripple Creek Personalities

OR A PLACE no larger than it was in its prime, the Cripple Creek Mining District has been able to claim an association with a rather impressive list of well-known persons. A few of them have been mentioned in previous chapters. Others, some better known, were also attracted to the area. But only a few among those who achieved later fame had come to dig for gold.

Otto Floto posted handbills in the town long before he became a reporter at *The Denver Post*. At the *Post* his colorful name was kited by one of the owners for the circus that the newspaper owned at the time. *The Denver Post* had acquired what became known as the Sells-Floto Circus, a name they used as a publicity vehicle for a number of years.

Vaudevillian Fred Stone was a stranded "hoofer," whose gymnast and clog act was a featured attraction at Cripple Creek's Ironclad Theatre. Edward Everett Horton, who later enjoyed a career as a comic in Hollywood films, was the piano player in a Cripple Creek theater, owned by the Moser family.

As a young man, Julius Marx, later known as Groucho Marx, drove a grocery wagon in the town of Victor. Tom Mix, one of Hollywood's premier Western actors, worked in his earlier years as a rider on one of the Cripple Creek cattle ranches. Since Tom Mix was a physically large man, he doubled as a bouncer each night, and on weekends, in Bennett Avenue saloons. A tall 22-year-old Jewish man named Bernard Baruch worked for a time as a pick and shovel miner in one of the Bull Hill mines. Like Tom Mix, he was powerfully built. At night, he earned money as a bare-knuckle fighter in various saloons. One night, he accepted a challenge, took on and defeated the boxing champion of the tough town of Altman. Baruch had a fine mind, too. He amassed a fortune on Wall Street and became the confidential financial advisor to every American president, from Woodrow Wilson to John F. Kennedy. Quite coincidentally, Baruch's father, Doctor Simon, performed the first operation for appendicitis in America.

The late big-time wrestler George Zaharias claimed Cripple Creek as home. He billed himself as the Galloping Greek from Cripple Creek. His wife, "Babe" Didrikson Zaharias, was a world-class athlete and golfer. Two Mormon brothers, in search of a wider and deeper rut, migrated up from the town of Manassa, in the San Luis Valley, to work as muckers in the Portland No. 1 mine. Their names were Bill and Jack Dempsey. When Jack was killed in a cave-in, brother Bill changed his name to Jack, and went on to become the heavyweight boxing champion of the world. He sometimes boxed at the prestigious Gold Coin Club in the Cripple Creek district.

Ford Frick, who later became America's first commissioner of baseball, was the reporter who covered Cripple Creek's events for the *Colorado Springs Telegraph.* "Texas" Guinan, the girl who billed herself as the "Toast of the Roaring '20's," got her start on a musical career playing the organ for a Sunday School class, in the town of Anaconda. Later, she opened a New York "speakeasy" and earned a measure of fame as the "Hello Sucker" girl.

In addition to the famed "Manassa Mauler," three other well-known boxers also fought at Cripple Creek. They were John L. Sullivan, Bob Fitzsimmons and James J. "Gentleman Jim" Corbett. Jack Johnson, our first black heavyweight champion, worked as a mucker in Cripple Creek's mines. He picked up extra money boxing in saloons at night.

Another graduate of Victor's high school was Damon Runyon, author of *Guys and Dolls,* and of many endearing and funny New York gangster stories. Two other notable itinerant visitors to Cripple Creek appeared in a previous chapter. "Soapy" Smith came up to Gillett in connection with Wolfe & Meadows' bull fight imbroglio. He operated games of chance at the bull ring. Carry Nation's visit was brief. She called Cripple Creek's Myers Avenue "A foul cesspool; the most lawless and wicked place to be found anywhere." She lamented publicly that Myers Avenue "...lured innocent men and women to death and destruction." Fortunately, for the

COLLECTION OF FRED AND JO MAZZULLA

WHEN THE Cripple Creek boom was on, Tom Mix worked as a bar-tender and bouncer in a Bennett Avenue saloon. Mix also worked as a cowboy on one of the early ranches.

COLLECTION OF FRED AND JO MAZZULLA

WILLIAM "JACK" DEMPSEY once worked as a mucker in one of Victor's mines. Sometimes he boxed at the Gold Coin Club.

WESTERN HISTORY DEPARTMENT – DENVER PUBLIC LIBRARY

RALPH CARR, one of Colorado's ablest governors, arrived in Victor from the Wet Mountain Valley. He also worked on a local newspaper and was a lifelong friend of Lowell Thomas.

WESTERN HISTORY DEPARTMENT – DENVER PUBLIC LIBRARY

FAMED JOURNALIST Lowell Thomas was a graduate of Victor's high school. He also cut his journalistic eye teeth on one of the newspapers in the district.

town, her stay was short. As noted previously, Carry Nation probably never even left the train. Nevertheless, she was in town long enough to account for her strong sentiments. George Pullman, the sleeping-car magnate, also visited Cripple Creek briefly.

Theodore Roosevelt was sent to Colorado in 1900 to campaign for William McKinley, who was not popular in the state. McKinley hoped that Roosevelt could win the support of "silver Republicans" and "anti-gold" Democrats. Postmaster Danny Sullivan arranged for Teddy to visit Cripple Creek and Victor. Although he was well received in Cripple Creek, he became the victim of an anti-McKinley protest in Victor. When things got ugly, Danny Sullivan grabbed a two by four and held off the demonstrators until Teddy reached the safety of his railroad coach. In gratitude, T.R. gave Danny a ring, which he wore and showed proudly for the rest of his life.

An almost entirely circumferential Cripple Creek attorney, named Jonah Maurice Finn, extracted a promise

FROM THE COLLECTION OF EVELYN AND ROBERT L. BROWN

THIS RARE CAMPAIGN BUTTON shows William Jennings Bryan, a three-time loser in the presidential sweepstakes and a visitor to Cripple Creek. The clock behind his head represents the 16 to 1 ratio between gold and silver that Bryan favored.

from Theodore Roosevelt to return as his house guest the following spring. Finn borrowed money to erect an opulent five-story mansion. Cripple Creekers called it "Finn's Folly." Upon his return, Roosevelt, now the U.S. vice president, called Finn's house "...The most beautiful home in Colorado." At a later time, the house was dismantled and moved to Lakewood. On his first visit, candidate Roosevelt came up on the Midland Terminal Railroad. But, as vice president in 1901, he rated a private car on the Short Line, exclaiming loudly that the "...scenery bankrupted the English language".

William Jennings Bryan, free-silver champion and a three-time loser in presidential races, also visited Cripple Creek. Bryan loved Colorado, and came here frequently. The following story came from one of his trips here from his native Nebraska. Its source was the late Thomas Hornsby Ferril, who was appointed Colorado's poet laureate by Governor Richard Lamm. One evening at the Denver Press Club, Ferril described how, as a cub reporter, he was sent to interview Bryan at the home where he was staying, on Denver's north side. Ferril and other reporters found Bryan moving vigorously to and fro on the front-porch swing. The reporters seated themselves on the porch railing. Ferril soon noticed that each time the statesman swung toward them, the reporters moved back in unison. Forward and back, the tableau continued. There were no deodorants at that time, and it was a blazing-hot day. Bryan's hands were clasped behind his head. Ferril insisted that the "Boy Orator of the Platte" had the most pungent case of B.O. he had ever encountered.

Spencer Penrose, a Cornishman by way of Pennsylvania, arrived in Cripple Creek in 1892. With his boyhood friend, Charles Tutt, Penrose amassed a vast fortune in Cripple Creek real estate, stocks and mines. Together, Tutt and Penrose also owned the rich C.O.D. mine, which they later sold at a handsome profit. Spencer Penrose and a few fun-loving pals were referred to as the "socialites." On one occasion, he and a lady companion rode horses into the barroom of the National Hotel and demanded that their mounts be served a mixed drink called a horse's neck. Penrose founded the Utah Copper Company in Bingham Canyon, Utah. It seemed that whatever he touched, turned to money. Today, his handsome mansion still stands in the Broadmoor area of Colorado Springs.

Yes, there were others worthy of note, but the foregoing will afford the reader with some idea of the notable persons who either lived in, or who visited, the great Colorado Gold Camp.

FROM THE COLLECTION OF EVELYN AND ROBERT L. BROWN

CARRY NATION, America's "vigilante in petticoats," began her career of saloon smashing at the age of 60. This portrait hangs in her former home at Medicine Lodge, Kansas.

ANTI-LIQUOR AND ANTI-TOBACCO crusader Carry Nation came to Cripple Creek to help reform notorious Myers Avenue. To finance her crusades, she sold miniature lapel pins.

FROM THE COLLECTION OF EVELYN M. BROWN

105

COLLECTION OF FREDA AND FRANCIS B. RIZZARI

IN THE BEGINNING this town was called Squaw Gulch. Later, it became Barry, and finally the name was changed to Anaconda.

A DISASTROUS FIRE in 1904 completely destroyed Anaconda. The wells were dry, and help came too late to save the town. Only the background hills, and the scar of the principal street remain.

FROM THE COLLECTION OF EVELYN AND ROBERT L. BROWN

View road continues on for another half mile to Midway, another family type town. Midway's name came from the notion that it was situated mid way between Cripple Creek and Victor. In common with Winfield, the mountain panorama to the west is spectacular. In fact, one of its "thirst quenchers" capitalized on the handsome mountain scenery, calling itself the Grand View Saloon. The Grand View building is gone now, but the large false-fronted structure, with the oddly placed windows, was also a saloon.

From Midway a trail turns east and reaches Altman in less than a mile. When last seen, this approach had been fenced off, so inquire locally before trespassing. A second approach to Altman is a steep four-wheel-drive road, which comes up past the Isabella mine, near Victor. Its current status is unknown.

As noted earlier, Altman was the union stronghold, and was a tough town. Since violence was so prevalent, Altman's undertaker offered group rates for funerals if the killing had occurred on Saturdays. At 10,700 feet, Altman was the highest town in the district. It never was the highest in the world, as some picture captions proclaimed. But at one time, it was the highest incorporated town in North America. Established on September 25, 1893, it also had schools, restaurants, retail stores, electricity, telephone service and many saloons. During the strike, "General" Jack Smith got drunk one night and attacked Altman single-handed. He freed several prison-

WESTERN HISTORY DEPARTMENT – DENVER PUBLIC LIBRARY

HERE IS ONE of the best pictures of Gillett. The scar at the picture's center would appear to be a cleared space for an extention of the principal street.

THIS 20th CENTURY color picture of Gillett shows how the highway cross-cuts the Gillett townsite without regard for the original street plat. The ridge behind the town is the back side of Pikes Peak.

FROM THE COLLECTION OF EVELYN AND ROBERT L. BROWN

FROM THE COLLECTION OF FRED AND JO MAZZULLA

OF ALL THE MINES at Cripple Creek, the Cresson probably came closest to fulfilling mankind's dream of a nest of pure gold.

WILLIAM H. JACKSON visited Altman at the turn of the century. His photograph shows a somewhat larger collection of structures at Altman.

FROM THE COLLECTION OF FRED AND JO MAZZULLA

AT ELKTON the Elkton Consolidated Mining & Milling Company's mill dominated the townsite. Behind the smoking stacks are the homes of Elkton's residents.

FROM THE COLLECTION OF EVELYN AND ROBERT L. BROWN

ALTHOUGH THE ELKTON MILL is gone, many of the homes still stand — empty now — at the base of Raven Hill. The fantastically rich Cresson mine was at Elkton.

FROM THE COLLECTION OF EVELYN AND ROBERT L. BROWN

ers in the jail before sobering up. Later, Smith was killed in an Altman saloon during a shoot-out with Marshal Jack Kelly. At its peak, between 1,800 and 2,000 persons called Altman home. Several surface buildings and mines can still be seen, when access is possible.

From Cripple Creek, an easy two-mile drive on paved Highway 67 will take you to the empty site of Anaconda. Horace Barry started the town as a cultural center in Squaw Gulch, and named it Barry in 1891. Later, it was known as Squaw Gulch, until the Anaconda mine was discovered. It already had a population of 500 in the year it was founded. It continued to grow until it was the fourth-largest town in the district by 1892. Two side-by-side streets ran down the gulch past a hardware store, the jail, law offices, a dressmaker's shop, saloons and assorted businesses, all of wooden construction. In addition to the Anaconda, the Dolly Varden and the huge Mary McKinney provided work for the men of the town. When the Mary McKinney was first discovered in 1898, the surface deposits were so rich that ox-drawn plows took out the gold. Its total production exceeded $11 million.

Just a few years ago, a man fell down the deep shaft of the Mary McKinney. The body has never been recovered. Anaconda's water supply was always poor. Dynamite had to be used to create fire breaks when a fire destroyed the town in 1904. After that, no effort was ever made to rebuild the town.

The scar that was Anaconda's principal street may be followed down the gulch for a half mile to the equally empty site of Mound City, a milling community, dating from 1891. It grew up around the Rosebud and the Brodie cyanide mills. In the beginning, the settlement was called Squaw Village. Judge Melville B. Gerry, who sentenced Alfred Packer for cannibalism in Lake City, served during his declining years as a jurist in Mound City. Five hundred people once lived here. Business houses included two meat markets, three grocery stores, two saloons, a clothing store, one hotel, a blacksmith and one barber shop. Curiously, Mound City was never platted or incorporated, and there were never any regular street patterns. After the Brodie mill was burned on August 9, 1902, most of the residents moved to Cripple Creek.

Just beyond the Carlton mill, on a hillside above Highway 67, is the well-preserved ghost town of Elkton. In common with Altman, it was a union town to such a degree that a company of the Colorado State militia was stationed here during the strikes. Two grocers, named Sam and George Bernard, located the Elkton mine and named the spot for a pair of shed elk antlers found on the ground beside the prospect hole. It produced over $13 million in gold. Cabins began to appear during the summer of 1893. Although there were four saloons, this was primarily a family town. The Sheldon Hotel and four others housed transients. Three grocery stores, two pharmacies, a book store and two physicians are listed in the 1900 Colorado Business Directory.

Elkton was always an easy place to get to since it was located on the lines of all three railroads and both interurban lines. The famous Cresson mine was located just a short distance above the town. Elkton's peak population was reached in 1905, when some 3,000 people lived there.

FROM THE COLLECTION OF EVELYN AND ROBERT L. BROWN

ALTMAN WAS KNOWN as the highest incorporated town in the world. Pikes Peak is part of the snow-covered range in the distance.

IN 1988 ALTMAN still retained some of its original buildings. The Pharmacist mine, in the foreground, produced $500,000 in gold.

FROM THE COLLECTION OF EVELYN AND ROBERT L. BROWN

ALTMAN, CRIPPLE CREEK DISTRICT, HIGHEST INCORPORATED TOWN IN THE WORLD

FROM THE COLLECTION OF EVELYN AND ROBERT L. BROWN

DURING THE 1894 STRIKE (see Chapter 11) this picture was made. The Colorado State Militia appears in the foreground, while Altman can be seen along the ridge above the tents.

ALTMAN'S ALTITUDE is 10,700 feet above sea level, making it the highest town in the Cripple Creek district. Located in a swale between Bull Hill and Bull Cliff, Altman once had a population of 2,500 persons. Pikes Peak is in the background of this picture.

COLLECTION OF EVELYN AND ROBERT L. BROWN – JAMES A. HARLAN PHOTO

FROM THE COLLECTION OF EVELYN AND ROBERT L. BROWN

FROM VICTOR a tunnel pierced a corner of Squaw Mountain to carry ores to be refined at the Economic Gold Extraction Company mill. The town of Eclipse grew up around the mill.

TODAY only the huge foundation of the Economic mill still identifies the site of the tiny settlement called Eclipse.

FROM THE COLLECTION OF EVELYN AND ROBERT L. BROWN

FROM THE COLLECTION OF EVELYN AND ROBERT L. BROWN

AT ONE TIME Anaconda was the fourth largest town in the Cripple Creek district. The huge cribbed dump on the hillside above the main street was from the Mary McKinney mine. Anaconda's main street was nearly a mile long and stretched back up the gulch toward Raven Hill. The photographer was Harry Buckwalter.

FOLLOWING THE FIRE, Anaconda was never rebuilt. The residents simply packed up and moved into Cripple Creek or Victor. The road that passes between the Mary McKinney and the empty townsite is Colorado Highway 67.

FROM THE COLLECTION OF EVELYN AND ROBERT L. BROWN

FROM THE COLLECTION OF EVELYN AND ROBERT L. BROWN

IN THIS VIEW of Mound City we see a false-front saloon that doubled as Judge Melville B. Gerry's court house. To its right is the Brody Cyanide Mill, which refined much of the more refractory ores from Stratton's properties.

THIS COLOR VIEW matches the angle of the Buckwalter photograph (above). Notice the scar at right, which marks the location of the Brody Cyanide Mill.

FROM THE COLLECTION OF EVELYN AND ROBERT L. BROWN

FROM THE COLLECTION OF EVELYN AND ROBERT L. BROWN

IN THE GULCH below Anaconda about 500 people lived in Mound City between 1891 and 1907. Curiously, Mound City never had a street plan. People simply built wherever they wished.

THIS PICTURE was taken in 1987. The road traversing the empty meadow was not a Mound City street. It bends around to the south to become a rather "hairy" four-wheel-drive trail.

FROM THE COLLECTION OF EVELYN AND ROBERT L. BROWN

In 1951, the Carlton mill was completed at a cost of $2 million. It still stands beside the highway, just below Elkton. A. E. Carlton purchased the Cresson mine for $4 million in 1916, and his mill refined much ore from the Cresson and other district mines. Arequa Gulch is directly below the Carlton mill, and is now nearly filled with the mill's tailings pond.

Arequa Gulch was the site of Bob Womack's original homestead. Ben Requa, an Italian, found the English pronunciation of his own last name difficult. "Arequa" was the best he could do. Others picked up on it, and it became the first settlement to be established in the district. It was just below Beacon Hill, and it dated from 1888. Arequa's streets were named for America's first several presidents. Whatever remains of the town is now deeply buried beneath the tailings pond.

These several mining settlements were representative of the towns that grew up adjacent to Cripple Creek.

FROM THE COLLECTION OF EVELYN AND ROBERT L. BROWN

HERE IS A CLOSE-UP VIEW of the Brody Cyanide Mill at Mound City. The multi-level structure to the right of the Brody mill was probably a boarding house for mill workers.

THIS RARE PICTURE of dogs, burros and people in front of a log grocery store was taken in Gillett. The tiny sign in the window above the burro's head advertises "Red Cross Cough Drops, 5¢ a box."

FROM THE COLLECTION OF FREDA AND FRANCIS B. RIZZARI

FROM THE COLLECTION OF EVELYN AND ROBERT L. BROWN

PIKES PEAK LOOMS up on the horizon behind a plume of smoke. The town is Goldfield. The tracks and overhead wires of the trolley line follow the principal street.

MATCHING THE OLDER PHOTOGRAPH of Goldfield and its electric-interurban line (above), this color picture shows majestic Pikes Peak and present-day Goldfield.

FROM THE COLLECTION OF EVELYN AND ROBERT L. BROWN

16

Victor and Its Neighbors

HROUGHOUT ITS HISTORY, Victor has been known as both the "City of Gold" and as the "City of Mines." While Cripple Creek was the district's largest community, Victor was second in size. A majority of the wealthy mining barons chose to live in Colorado Springs or Cripple Creek, but most of their mines were adjacent to Victor. Quite naturally, there was, and still is, a rivalry. Victor's Gold Coin mine was found near the middle of the town, while a crew was digging the foundation for a hotel. It was Frank Woods who hit the 20 inch Gold Coin vein under Diamond Avenue. It paid off at $50,000 per month.

Sam Strong's rich mine was just behind the railroad depot. Both of the Portlands and Stratton's Independence were close by, on Battle Mountain, as were several of the district's largest producers. Mine tunnels honeycomb much of the land under Victor's streets. Consequently, people were able to get rich by putting down shafts in their own back yards. In 1936, Victor realized $5,000 from processing low-grade ore that had been used to pave the street in front of the post office.

A majority of Victor's best mines were discovered in 1891 and 1892. Actually, Victor was built on the site of the rich Mount Rosa Placer. Harry, Frank and Warren Woods had gained mining experience at Kokomo, Robinson and Leadville prior to forming the Woods Investment Company, which developed Victor in 1893. Building lots were free to businessmen, but $25 to everyone else. One source insists that Victor's population once reached nearly 25,000, with fine homes, three newspapers, several hotels and five churches. It had both railroad and interurban trolley service. About 60 trains and electric interurbans passed through the town each day.

Irish Jimmy Doyle served as mayor of Victor during the 1890's. Doyle and his partner, Jimmy Burns, had discovered and owned the great Portland No. 1 and No. 2, named for their hometown of Portland, Maine. Doctor Harry Thomas, father of Lowell Thomas, was the town's physician. Although Victor's population was a modest 265 in the last census, today's visitor will find much to see, do and photograph. A visit to Victor is easily worth the easy six-mile drive from Cripple Creek.

Nearby Goldfield, hardly a stone's throw from Victor, was platted on January 8, 1895. It already had 3,500 people by 1901, making it the district's third-largest community. As owners of the two Portland mine properties, Doyle and Burns established Goldfield as a residence center for their employees. A City water and sewer system were finished by 1896. Because the terrain here was relatively flat, all three railroads maintained depots and freight yards in the town. In common with Altman and Elkton, Goldfield was another strong union town, as well as a center for families. When the strike was broken, and union men were deported from the district, Goldfield was left without a mayor or any member of its town council.

Goldfield had many saloons. The one owned by Mother Duffy was undoubtedly the most famous. In an earlier chapter her establishment of the first Sunday School was mentioned. Goldfield has often boasted of having the longest continuously operating Sunday School in the area, quite an unusual claim for a mining town.

Apparently Mother Duffy was quite religious — in her own crude way. Whenever an itinerant clergyman reached the town, Mrs. Duffy would close her establishment to drinking. Two large bed sheets were kept on a shelf behind the bar. One was used to drape across the saloon art, while the second covered the bar, which now became the pulpit. The "professor" (pianist) played the usual hymns on his piano, and Mother Duffy's "girls" came downstairs to double as the choir. Her saloon patrons sang lustily and tapped their feet, while Mother Duffy's trombone voice rendered the "amens."

Communion wine was never a problem at Duffy's place. Following the service, the bar was re-opened for the thirsty congregation. Church services were good for the saloon business. The practice of holding religious services in saloons was abandoned after more conventional houses of worship were established.

Macon was the first name adopted for the town of Independence. It was located just up the hill to the north of Goldfield. It took its name from its proximity to Stratton's Independence mine. Actually, the town was nestled in a valley between the lower slopes of Bull Hill and Bull Cliff, about a mile below Altman. Independence was founded on November 11, 1894. Its town limits included the earlier site of Hull City and the rich Hull City Placer. The Vindicator mine, dynamited by Harry Orchard, was located in the Montgomery Gulch section of the town.

In common with its neighbors, Independence was always a family place. It had few stores. Shoppers merely walked down the hill to Goldfield or over to Victor.

Beyond Goldfield and Independence was the valley of Grassy Creek, the site of a tiny settlement, called "Gassy." Allen Gullion, an original settler, was the source of this unflattering name. It was bestowed on the place by Gullion's neighbors, who deplored his annoying flatulence. Later, more sensitive settlers insisted that the name be changed to Grassy. Other homesteaders, even more discreet, changed the name to Cameron in 1900.

Cameron Avenue, the principal street, was 80 feet wide. Here, the Woods brothers built Pinnacle Park, the area's only amusement park. An elaborate overpass allowed people to cross the busy railroad tracks safely on their way to the park. It had a baseball field, family picnic area, a dance pavilion and a small zoo. Stone remnants of the lion cages may be seen back in the trees, above the road.

On the other side of Victor, the Woods boys built the Economic Gold Extraction Company chlorination mill. A really tiny village, called Eclipse, grew up around the mill to house its workers. Eclipse and its mill existed because Victor's Gold Coin mine was almost in the middle of the town, and a large tailings dump was growing beside it. So, the Woods brothers drilled a 3,700 foot-long tunnel, called either the United Mine Tunnel or the Columbine-Victor Tunnel. It pierced Squaw Mountain in 1899, and carried ore for processing out of Victor. Teddy Roosevelt viewed this complex in 1901 and pronounced it "Bully!" The Economic mill burned in 1908. Sparks and flames spread across Eclipse and destroyed most of the workers' homes. The mill's foundation and tunnel openings can be seen below the highway, on the last curve before you enter Victor.

There were a few other suburbs, too, obscure places like Lawrence, Hollywood, Portland and Dutchtown. Eventually, Victor absorbed all of them.

FROM THE COLLECTION OF EVELYN AND ROBERT L. BROWN

IN A HAPPIER TIME, a brass marching band led this parade along one of Goldfield's streets. Note the wavy wooden sidewalk in front of the church and the Goldfield city hall, in the left background.

THE ANGLE of this picture matches that of the older Goldfield parade picture (above). One home and the city hall are still there.

FROM THE COLLECTION OF EVELYN AND ROBERT L. BROWN

FROM THE COLLECTION OF EVELYN AND ROBERT L. BROWN

FROM A POINT on Big Bull Mountain, a photographer recorded this panorama of Goldfield when it was the third largest community in the Cripple Creek district.

HERE, IN VIEW, are three "short beer" checks from saloons in the family town of Goldfield.

COLLECTION OF EVELYN AND ROBERT L. BROWN

124

FROM THE COLLECTION OF FRED AND JO MAZZULLA

HULL CITY grew up around the Hull City Placer. At first, it was annexed by Goldfield. At a later time, it became a part of Independence.

BOTH EQUESTRIANS and pedestrians of the Colorado State Militia are shown in Hull City at the time of the 1894 strike.

COLLECTION OF EVELYN AND ROBERT L. BROWN

The Bowl of Gold in The 20th Century

N COMMON WITH so many of Colorado's other mountain towns, there have been far-reaching changes in both the economy and the population base of the Cripple Creek country. Several rather obvious factors have contributed to the district's decline.

First of all, America's monetary system was based on bimetalism — utilizing both gold and silver — for most of the 19th century. Then, the U.S. adopted a full gold standard, from 1900 until 1933. In 1934 a Gold Reserve Act was passed by Congress, and America has been on a modified gold standard ever since, although gold is no longer used as a medium of exchange. Inevitably, taking gold coins out of circulation as legal tender decreased the need for that metal.

Another vexing problem was the fact that $20 an ounce was the going rate for gold at the time of Cripple Creek's best years. It increased to $35 an ounce during Franklin D. Roosevelt's "New Deal" years. But those times also brought long-needed mining and safety restrictions, which made gold extraction far more costly. Prevailing union wage scales, Social Security, the national minimum wage and the inflated costs of nearly everything, from dynamite to miners' picks and shovels, added to the expenses of an already risky enterprise.

Early gold recovery at Cripple Creek came from ores close to the surface, which were easier to extract. Deep mining is far more costly, necessitating complex milling processes, extensive and expensive tunneling, motorized lifts (elevators) that can take workers far underground, as well as powerful fans to dispel bad air and ventilate the tunnels, and many other 20th century innovations.

Mining costs escalate sharply as shafts go deeper into the Earth. Underground water is an added probability. In 1910, the Roosevelt Tunnel was completed. It drained the mines for nearly 20 years. The 17 mile long Carlton Tunnel was finished in 1941. It drained off water to a depth of nearly 7,000 feet. It had cost $1,250,000 to complete. Cripple Creek's Carlton Tunnel should not be confused with the 10,700 foot high Busk-Ivanhoe Tunnel, renamed the Carlton Tunnel at a later time. It was built for the Colorado Midland Railroad to connect Leadville with Basalt and the Western Slope of Colorado. It was used for automobile traffic in the 1920-1930 years, but it is now abandoned.

America's involvement in the second World War resulted in a nearly total shut-down of mining in the entire district. The rising costs of labor, mining machinery, explosives, railroad transportation and freight placed a heavy burden on the business of gold extraction. Likewise, the price of smelter services soared, while the dollar value of gold remained fixed by law. After the peace, rampant inflation dictated only very limited mining enterprises, unless costs could be held in line, and that rarely happened. Even more seriously, the price for gold was still pegged at $35 an ounce. Currently, with gold prices seeking their own level in a fluctuating market, the price varies between $300 and $500 for an ounce. Despite this, many mines, which contain large deposits of deep gold, cannot operate profitably.

What of Cripple Creek's future? During the summer, the tourist business has been quite good for a number of years. Interesting new shops open for business on Bennett Avenue each season. Colorado Springs' Golden Cycle Corporation continues to purchase available mining properties as they come on the market, looking toward the time when the demand for gold, and gold prices make mining profitable once more, in this bowl that Midas touched.

As a consequence of the election of 1990, voters approved the introduction of limited gambling for some of Colorado's hard-pressed mountain communities, including Cripple Creek and Victor. With proper regulation, it is hoped that gambling may provide a needed shot in the arm for the economy.

This, then, has been the story of Cripple Creek, in both text and pictures. It was the last and easily the greatest Rocky Mountain bonanza, the gold strike that held Colorado's shattered economy together during the difficult times that followed the Silver Panic of 1893. We may never see its like again.

BIBLIOGRAPHY

Cafky, Morris, *Rails Around Gold Hill*. Rocky Mountain Railroad Club, Denver, 1955.

Chadbourne, Robert, *Cripple Creek War – August, 1904*. The Denver Westerners Roundup – April, Denver, 1971.

Dorsett, Phyllis Flanders, *The New Eldorado*. The Macmillan Co., New York, 1970.

Eberhart, Perry, *Guide to the Colorado Ghost Towns and Mining Camps*. Sage Books, Chicago, 1959.

Griswold, Don and Jean, *Colorado's Century of Cities*. The Authors, Denver, 1958.

Holbrook, Stewart, *The Rocky Mountain Revolution*. Henry Holt and Co., New York, 1956.

Lee, Mabel Barbee, *Cripple creek Days*. Doubleday & Co., Garden City, New York, 1958.

Lee, Mabel Barbee, *Back in Cripple Creek*. Doubleday & Co., Garden City, New York, 1958.

Lee, W. Storrs, *Colorado, a Literary Chronicle*. Funk and Wagnalls, New York, 1970.

Mazzulla, Fred and Jo, *The First 100 Years*. The Authors, Denver, 1956.

Melrose, Frances, *Rocky Mountain Memories*. Denver Publishing Co., Denver, 1986.

Ormes, Robert, *Tracking Ghost Railroads in Colorado*. Century One Press, Colorado Springs, 1976.

Paul, Rodman, *Mining Frontiers of the Far West*. Holt, Rinehart and Winston, New York, 1963.

Rastall, B. M., *The Cripple Creek Strike of 1893*. Colorado College Studies, Colorado Springs, 1905.

Sprague, Marshall, *Money Mountain*. Little Brown & Co., Boston, 1953.

Sprague, Marshall, *Newport in the Rockies*. Little Brown & Co., Boston, 1953.

Taylor, Robert Guilford, *Cripple Creek Mining District*. Filter Press, Palmer Lake, Colorado, 1973.

Waters, Frank, *Midas of the Rockies*. University of Denver Press, Denver, 1949.

Williams, Albert N., *Rocky Mountain Country*. Duell, Sloan & Pearce, New York, 1950.

Wolfe, Doris, *The Gold Camp Road*. The Author, Colorado Springs, 1988.

Wolle, Muriel Sibell, *Stampede to Timberline*. The Author, Boulder, Colorado, 1949.